Will Work For Peace

New Political Poems

Brett Axel, Editor

Zeropanik Press
Trenton NJ
1999

Zeropanik Press
PO BOX 1565
Trenton, NJ 08607-1565
zpanik@voicenet.com

Back cover photograph taken by Miriam Axel-Lute

Thanks are given to the following organizations for their
support in this project: A Gathering of the Tribes, Go Poetry,
Zuzu Petals, and The Austin Poetry Map.

Printed in the USA by Morris Press
3212 Highway 30 Kearney, NE 68847

Artists Proof Edition
First Printing
1999

Submissions of new political poems for a possible second edition
of *Will Work For Peace* may be sent directly to the editor,
Brett Axel, 11 Wickham Avenue, Middletown, NY 10940

Visit Brett Axel on the internet at http://www.orn.net/~axels/welcome.htm

ISBN 0-9666459-1-X

There were weak bonds to me, if any, in my family of birth. As an adult, I have met a few individuals that I have developed strong bonds to. They are the family of my choice and I love them unconditionally.

My cousin, Miriam Axel-Lute, is both a member of my family of birth and a member of my family of choice.

On November 22nd, 1998, Miriam and I participated in a demonstration in Columbus Georgia, imploring our government to close the US Army's School of the Americas where we have trained and empowered Latin American dictators to commit atrocities against their poor civilian population. It was there that I wrote and held the sign 'Will Work For Peace' which would become the title of this book. Miriam took the photograph that is now on the back cover.

Although I was a guest at her parent's wedding before she was born, this was only the second time we had met. Now, I cannot imagine a time when we did not have each other.

This book is dedicated to Miriam Axel-Lute, to all of our families of birth and all of our families of choice and to the day when this encompasses everyone.

Brett Axel

Introduction

It is seldom that so many poets of our time cross boundaries of land, of sea, and of mind, to come together for any reason. In *Will Work For Peace*, they have done just that for the best of reasons: to express their outrage over converging injustices in the world.

Inspired by an array of inequities that surround us, these poems pull no punches while addressing a variety of issues ranging from the imprisonment of Mumia Abu-Jamal to Chiapas, the attempted impeachment of President Bill Clinton to AIDS, ecology, poverty, discrimination, and of course, war, peace, violence and non-violence. The poets themselves come from vastly different approaches, every continent, and many social and economic backgrounds. One is 89 years old, another just 16; all united by a command of the English language and the desire for a better world. Since all social change starts with an idea and poets plant the seeds from which ideas grow, we need these poets and we this need book.

I'd like to see *Will Work For Peace* given to every school child. It is for them, as the heirs to the world we are creating—and for the adults who, in the spirit of this poetry, can help to change the way we live. If everyone who is touched by this book makes the commitment, that these 144 poets have; that they, too, *Will Work For Peace*, we won't just be working for peace, we will have it.

Steve Cannon

Will Work For Peace

Will work for peas,
will work for grease,
from old bones
in garbage soup.
Will work for a place to pee
where it ain't against the law
to take a whizz.
Will work for peanuts in the zoo,
caged in, not out,
a sign around my neck,
CRACK ADDICT WITH HIV.
This is what it looks like
when you ain't got no hundred dollar blouse.

Arupa Chicrini

Mother's Book:
found poem

"Mother's Book", 1831,
knows best.
The use of flannel-drawers,
provoking irritation,
is useful for inviting
the flow of the menses.
We should advise
gymnastic exercises,
walking and riding,
the games of battledore.
At last resort,
leeches to the vulva.
Menstrual exaltation!

Home economics textbook, 1954,
knows best.
Have dinner ready.
Most men are hungry when they come
home.
Prepare yourself.
Put a ribbon in your hair and be fresh
looking.
His boring day may need a lift.
Prepare the children-
they are little treasures
and he would like to see them
playing the part.
Greet him with a warm smile.
Make him comfortable.
Suggest that he lie down in the bedroom.
Let him talk first.

Try to understand his world of strain and
pressure.
Make the evening his.
There will be a test!

Bloomingdale's christmas catalog, 1996,
knows best.
Treat your little ones to a treasure
for hours of make-believe fun.

Our boy's trunk includes
hat and play knife in pouch,
bandanna and vest,
and saber and eyepatch.
Our girl's trunk includes
a silver tiara,
pink satin conical hat,
lavender glitter cap-sleeve leotard,
rainbow net tutu with rose buds,
solid pink boa,
pink glitter cape,
mock pearl necklace,
and tape of the 12 Dancing Princesses
story.
Or order our newest Barbie:
CK gray crop top, and
black bra and panties.
All American made by A Wish come True!

Alix Olson

Irish Cows

Irish cows aren't Catholic or Protestant,
don't know where the borders are, or care.

I had to stop in Doolin, to breathe the air
sweet-scented with their breath

and say hello to cows, where they pressed
together as their nature dictates, against

the narrow street. The ample nearness
of their sloping sides, like bowed staves

of Viking craft amidships, pleases, heaving bulk
rough greeny tongues and square pink noses,

sounds of grass being ground into milk
– that fine domestic alchemy – and the lowing.

I'd missed them, i suppose. My last trip home,
driving south along the coast of Florida, I'd thought,

Not a lot of cows, but with a man I've known
since we were children, the word I chose

was *cattle*. In childhood cattle all are cows. Clouds
brought to earth, they hovered near the house at night,

friendly presences in jasmine-scented dark
that painted out the fence. Elbows on the sill

of cool ceramic, I'd watch Santiago, Brahman bull
whose white drape dappled with gray shadow

was the color of the banyan tree in town
and from the same place, another set of roots

in foreign sand. Mary Beth asked my church
behind the eighth-grade barracks where we sang

a range of music sacred and profane, carols,
mindless patriotic songs, the heartbreak

we would know as we grew older. White children
rendered spirituals that told of slavery

in six-part harmony, and every year "Red River Valley;"
none of us had had a lover, none

had ever seen a river wider than the slow Myakka
I looked up from planting fruit or flowers, said

Synagogue – or maybe *Jew* – and vivid as this very day:
My momma won't let me play with heathen!

She throws her hoe onto the sand and stomps away
leaving me bewildered in the garden.

Connemara farmers drive their cattle to the sea
make them swim against their nature and the tides

to offshore islands where the grazing's sweeter.
Head to angled bony hip, bumping, clumped together,

the herd struggles, heaves and slides. Steam rises
from their hides, they gain purchase on the stony verge, find

8

aromatic grass and clover. Cattle once were currency in Eire;
still they're bartered, used for gifts and bride-price: trade

in cattle even now bears memories of the sacred.
Ungainly and unbeautiful, heavy with milk and meat

they meander over the land. It would seem that dread
is not a part of their equipment. Irish cattle remind

me of a time bound to a place, and easy laughter;
I envy how they go, unknowing to the slaughter.

Deena Linett

Pinaud's Tonic

Five disabled dollars later, this man is cleansed—
Briefly allowed to borrow some human sunlight
On another stranger's bench.

His heart is now as hard as a claymore,
Pointed at some forgotten enemy,
Beating eight to the bar like some slopehead jukebox,
Pulsing with the bagged donations
Of o-positive neighbors back home.

The barber sweeps away
The remnants of this man's raincatchers;
He knows how close they were
To being brothers to the dragon—
He has breathed its jellied fire before;
He shut that door with a shiny trade school license,
His talk gets smaller as the years allow.

For six hungry weeks, this man
Could be Westmoreland himself,
Safe in the knowledge
That anyone could love him;
He could limp and clang with the best of fatted Rotarians,

Eating the center of the rubber chicken
Every Monday at twelve.

His neck stiffens in the breeze
With the steady burn of Pinaud's Tonic,
He has become temporary master of all he can remember,
He rises to greet his brethren with a one-legged kiss,
He embraces the illusions of a town that evaded him.

(I gave him a cup of water and he spilled it all over the place.)

Michael Pollick

The Coalition

If among earth's kings lord Gilgamesh should remain unreasonable,
if civility refuses to assume citizenship between the rivers,
Sir Agamemnon will assemble a diligent Protestant coalition

to administer appropriate slaughter as correction and discipline.
He will station responsible King Herod with his updated hoplites
backed by Xin the Emperor's stolid terracotta battalions

beside Mercury, Mars, and Athena from the province of Olympus
to persuade by the rhetoric of atrocity and abomination.
Young Colonel Bonaparte, upgrading to Alexander, will distribute

massacre by African blowguns, by tortoises from Cipango, by
whinnying helicopters from the stables of Atilla, and by Cyclopean missiles.
By Greek fire he will melt the Saracen who thinks to flourish a scimitar.

If Lord Gilgamesh should remain unreasonable, the coalition
will incinerate retreating Uruki soldiers, furthering the projects
of Pharaoh Death, President Death, Shogun Death, Imperator Death.

Donald Hall

Black, not Hispanic

I lament the lack of Spanish on my tongue
like a pregnant woman's cravings on an August
night when the belly is too big for the car and
hot is alive in every swollen joint.

I remember my Mother changing her mind about my color
when I was ten. I was Black. The next day, I was Hispanic.
She talked of Panama –
    a slip of land that looked like my Daddy
colored Grandmothers. I checked the box marked Black

anyway. She couldn't see me. I had not changed since
the time I was four when I was informed firmly about
my Blackness. It made sense back then. The word coffee
has a startling intensity and jolting blood electricity.

My Grandmother tells her life in a rolling sequence
of Intelligentsia identity.
Dates her events along name-calling fashions. In eighty years,
she has been as many flavors of Black as Baskin & Robbins
serves ice cream. South Africa told her

She was White once, when they needed her not to be Black
for eleven days. That story was funny enough for me to want
to stay Black when I was ten. The "in crowd"
served up diversity on the fancy platters of multi-culturalism.
I remember when rainbows

were about God's promise. Instead of a buzz word
stinging like any insect with venom for your veins.
My tongue tangos and salsas. Limbos deftly
under the Queen's English. My Grandmother tongue

was snipped out. Efficient as runaway slave-breaking
techniques. How many languages can they beat out?
How many times will we deny ancestors? Certainly
more than Peter Rome was an infant dabbling at Empire.

I lament the lack of Spanish on my tongue.
This dance of definitions has become tiring.

I no longer wish to try on names as if
our port of entry was a chic boutique now past its time

and worthy of mourning. One slave name
honors my ancestors. The other maintains an illusion
that we are who colonized us rather
than families of Africans divided by a new world.
These definitions clank and howl.

I hear them like moans bounced off the stench
of ship holds when we fed the Atlantic new salt.

Christina Springer

Gray-blue sunlight specks
off bomb casing that is
the Republican's head, ricochets
depth futile with birthplaces
of the opposition engulfed by
raw cancellation demonstrated to be

inevitable. The candidate has
sponsored a huge hole on
the corner to tighten tongues while
in his own apartment Lefty was
ventilated by two bullets silent
as voters. Unspoken memorials

participate in departure, ambivalent
thoughts wired to ownerless
fence with permission or
advice; "go in peace, Lefty,"
meaning

please do not hang around
here after you are dead --but

everyone on Loisada goes
in peace you stinking
animal spit begs to say

12

after life won hour to
hour is stripped off by
total eclipse

the missing front door lock
place of thorough punishment
blank on paperwork moved
over by pen tip that drains
name of the deceased.

Paul Skiff

Pocahontas Grants An Interview With *Rolling Stone*

How did you hear about the role?
Disney wanted to resurrect an American Legend, as far as my agent told
me, a real historical female heroine, none of that hackney Brother Grimm
crap. Betsy Ross was their first choice but the editors had a hard time
making a musical out of stars and shit. The scoop is they wanted Helen
Keller but she couldn't sing or dance.

Did you know that you'd get the role?
Sacajawea was considered but it would've taken the staff too long to
research her trail. Being on a tight budget, it was easier for them to stay in
Jamestown and take notes for a month.

What did you have to do to get the role?
I forgot my image would be on moccasins, coffee jugs, and dolls. As soon
as I did my screen test and wardrobe had me try on my costume, execs said
I had to lose weight and hired a physical trainer to give me a "Baywatch"
figure. A stylist designed me a weave, super jet black extensions to add a
dramatic effect when I ran through the hidden pine trails of the forests.
Those extensions are now patented and you could purchase extensions for
all sizes and colors at Bloomingdales. Each extension is carefully hand-
woven by my tribe and contains .5% of my own hair and a portion of the
profits will go for Pocaloca Land, a camping resort where kids can pick
berries and meet white people settlers.

How strenuous was the role?
It was really awkward, running barefoot in a hoochie skirt. I wore skins
my whole life but I'd gotten so used to wearing denims and a cotton-T.

13

Shooting on location was cold. It took 16 hours to do "The Colors Of The Wind" shoot and I mean I had to belt my tits off.

What was Mel Gibson like playing John Smith?
I was nervous working with Mel and it was difficult reliving that part of my life. I have to admit, I was an out-of-control teen but I never got into John Smith.

Are there any eligible Hollywood men in your future?
The love of my life is John Rolfe and my son. Honestly, the only reason I took the part was because I thought they'd tell my story: A Powhatan princess dying of small pox in a Coney Island circus. They wanted a singing Wonder Woman who'd dodge speeding tomahawks to save a man bland as succotash. I'm not bionic. When you boil it all down, I'm just a maiden kayaking through life with the humming birds and otters.

What are your upcoming projects?
I'm opening the ribbon-cutting ceremony for the Pocahontas log cabin ride at EuroDisney and I've been offered the part in the musical theater version of "Dances With Wolves" on Broadway and George C. Wolfe wants me to do "Bring in Da T-Pee, Bring in Da Funk."

                                                              Regie Cabico

---

Advice from a Lotto Agent

Some say it is only luck
the way the numbers
fall down the tubes;
there are arguments
against such an irrational thing.
Play the zeroes when the temperature drops,
and watch for the fives,
they're wicked when they double up.
Play the same numbers everyday, every year,
they'll hit big at the eclipse
in the seventh month
of the right decade,
blessed with the sweat of the gods.
Then rip up the old tickets
and throw them in the trash,
leave them there a few days—
pick them out

and tape them back together,
by that time, they'll be seasoned
with the luck they need.
Finally, always go with the goofs
some Lotto agent made,
however bad it may be,
chances are it was under
someone else's control.

James Ruffini

Christmas

Rudolph the red nosed reindeer, you'll go down in history.
Too bad you did not!
Too bad history books don't reserve space for stupid talking animals
too bad no one even knows what year you supposedly "*saved christmas*"
too bad that in order for Santa Claus to really exist he would have to deliver
    presents to 100,000 families a second
too bad that even if he *could* move this fast it would be impossible for him to
    be as fat as he is
if Santa Claus were really coming to town it might be a good idea to hide all
    of the egg mcmuffins
Santa is the only fat guy in history people actually *like*. It doesn't matter that
    he's a big fat slob. Everyone *hates* all of the other really fat people.
one time me and my girlfriend saw a really fat guy with a dog and a sign
pushing a shopping cart down 5th avenue near 42nd street. The sign said,
"please have sex with me" and that's all the guy said. Please have sex with
me, ladies, will somebody have sex with me
he was dirty and he was fat and everyone hated him!
Nobody even looked at him
His dog certainly didn't know what was happening
at one point the man introduced himself
will somebody please have sex with me
my name is Teddy *I will be your bear*
your name may be Teddy but you will not be my bear
it actually wasn't that bad of a pickup line
none of this has anything to do with the existence of Santa Claus
I once heard a theory that there were actually hundreds of Santa Clauses
and that all of the elves were former Santa Clauses
the reason they got so small was because of all the calories they burned

going from house to house each night

I once tricked a guy into believing that I am Australian and that there is
  no Santa Claus in Australia

it could be said that there is a different Santa each year and that once they
 get to be Santa Claus

after they get small all they can do is help out the next guy

which brings up the idea of Presidents

after you are President what the hell are you going to do with the rest
  of your life?

I suppose you could be a great humanitarian like Jimmy Carter but what
   about Reagan and Bush?

What did they do besides getting Alzheimer's and playing golf?

One time Ronald Reagan was in Las Vegas receiving a big award for his
wonderful environmental preservation policy

Some guy who must have realized that Reagan didn't have any good
environmental preservation policies stormed onto the stage, *smashed*
Reagan's crystal award trophy and said "excuse me president Reagan!"

we all waited for what he was going to say next

standing up for the true environmentalists of the world but the next thing
he knew he had been tackled by four security guards. He tasted podium!

One wonders why the awards ceremony was in Las Vegas

after that one wonders what happened to the man

I played the footage over and over again

excuse me president Reagan

I turned the volume up really high, and muffled, underneath the suits and
 bullet proof vests:

my name is teddy i will be your bear

it was teddy!! teddy saved the day!! during this holiday, I plead with you
to please have sex with this great American hero known as sweet Teddy.

                                                              Keystone

---

Not Within Me

I can not help but look past the blackness of my skin,
past the flesh and blood cells,
past the working organs of my body–
I find there is no nigger within me.
only a man.
Though it may exist

16

the only evidence of its being
is the blackness printed on a white sheet
pressed between the covers
of my dictionary.

Jim Eve

It Comes Out in the Wash

The World has seen
Pinochet's Dreams
while dead-Spaniards
dance a head-less
foxtrot.
and they are quiet.
the violin is
playing itself
among the ashes.

Fletch

Dismath

The trouble with communism is
Theres only one pete seeger
The trouble with capitalism is
Theres more than one donald trump
The trouble with religion is
There are far far far too many clergy
The trouble with politicians is
Not one of them nor all of them together
Can stop that multiheaded creature
Communism capitalism clergy
From leeching off the struggling
Beleaguered working people
And the trouble with art is
There are far too few practitioners.

Tusay

November

The Ash tree weeps
The last of Her leaves
Unto your corpse.
He lynched you—
Upside down,
Removing your skin of Motherhood,
Peeled violently!
From your hind quarters;
Rolled up like a whore's skirts
As he prepares to enter you
With his survival knife...
When you suckled the yearling,
could your Sisters have imagined this?
Hanging, suspended
By this pernicious, male inquisition,
Above the rock, Like the Rock...
And these yankee bastards
Grope through tick infested grasses
For one more kill...
One more chance
To cut the nipples of Motherhood;
Guillotine a herd master...
You hang!
You hang!
Clothes line girdles
the Soul of Ash witness. Listen now!
To Vulture conversation...
Grisly invocation of selfish Crows
Flapping through weeds;
To the adulations of grim
Hunters taunting the imprisoned hound
As He wails ice crystals in Crow weather,
The only dirge at your incomplete Wake...

Robert Milby

The Difference between breasts and tits

Women have breasts
Chicks have tits
Breasts are admired
Tits get no respect
Breasts nurse
Tits are as barren as Barbie
Breasts nurture
Tits compete
Breasts seduce
Tits tease
Breasts make love
Tits fuck
Breasts are caressed
Tits get sucked
Breasts adorn bodies
Tits fill bras
Eventually, breasts sag
Tits get siliconed
Breasts weep
Tits whine
Breasts come in all shapes and sizes
Tits better be just so
Rubens glorifies breasts
Playboy airbrushes tits
The Madonna has breasts
Madonna has tits
Breasts accept
Tits wish they were somewhere else
Breasts are wise
Tits don't know any better
Breasts survive
Tits wither
Breasts rule
Tits say, "Yes, sir!"

In the end, of course,
Breasts will have the last laugh
and tits?
Tits just don't get the joke

                                        Lisa Martinovic

Toy Soldiers

my daddy bought me a thousand toy soldiers
and i play with them whenever i'm alone.
sometimes in the early morning light
i arrange them in infantries
along the ridges and valleys of my bed sheets
sending hundreds to their death
in the cauldron of wrinkles and folds.
someday i'm going to shoot my enemies
that's what my daddy tells me.
now me and my buddies
go rat a tat tat
and somebody falls down
but they're only fooling.
anyway i prefer playing with my soldiers.
sometimes i fight the battle of gettysburg
over and over on my bed
arranging the blanket
like devil's den
or cemetery ridge.
i get a lot of satisfaction
watching rebels fall.
this is more fun
than dancing with all those silly girls.
someday i'll be smarter than everybody
and have a big farm in pennsylvania
and hire some immigrants
to re-enact the battle of iwo jima.
but now i play alone
with my soldiers
while nobody's looking
in the privacy of my room
i can kill anyone.

bruce weber

Waiting in Post Office Line

If you had noticed me
waiting my post office customer turn
caught in suspended animation

you might have mistaken
stoic demeanor for patience.

If you were a curious person
you'd follow my gaze
to government pamphlets

harmlessly inked on innocent paper
white as a baby's baptism gown.

If you were observant,
looking through my eyes
you'd see ugly ominous meanings
disguised as patriotic words of duty:
"Selective Service and You."

If you were being me
you would shiver from chilling draft
stirring lifetimes of memory dust devils
cycloning holocaust ashes.
Mental maternal mutiny
would rage against infernal machine
that swallows young men whole
spitting out soldiers
for sacrifice
to insatiable war minotaur.

And while you were me
recalling the instant of agony
followed by ecstasy
birthing your son
you would commit
private acts of reason
and treason against
war mongering men and their minions –
miniature men writing government pamphlets.

You might have noticed me
stoically step out of line.

                                        Stazja McFadyen

Pork

This little piggy
    freed the market
       so this
little worker
    lost his home

This little piggy
    cornered roastbeef
       so this
little family
    had none

And this little piggy lied
    WE   WE   WE   ALL THE WAY!
      in his speeches   in his columns   in his homes
in his mirrors   in his cups
    and even in his pomes

                                Joel Chace

The Easy Way

There are two ways to win a poetry slam:
Tell people what they want to hear–
that's the easy way–
or tell people what they need to hear–
that's HARD.
It's easier to find the mob in each person
than to find each person in the mob.
You think you're righteous because you're popular?
Listen, the best slammer of the century
started in small beer halls and on the street,
wherever he could find ears– and people
listened and cheered, first five or six, then 30, hundreds,
thousands, MILLIONS hung on his every word like
flies on shit as he screamed, whispered, spit words
like bullets, burned, banshee-wailed, smiled like acid, turned
reasonable, tender, eloquent, heroic,
telling the People that beneath their sullen inertia
were heroes in hiding, ramrod destinies, telling them
of blood, roots, love of one's people, how degenerates and

wimps in power were corrupting their children,
how international bankers ruined their nation, how professors
were whores, how sacrifice and hard work led to freedom, how men
must be bold and women must be strong to make room in the world
for their children, how the People must be pure of heart and
unbending as they rise up against their oppressors
and crush them underfoot like vipers or venomous insects—
and he gave them targets they could SEE, enemies close at hand
who could not fight back, the ones his People
had already learned to love to hate.
Oh, a few old elitists and nit-picky intellectuals and
namby-pampy priests attacked and mocked while they could,
but the People, the millions loved him more than the loved
their parents, spouses, children— chanted his name,
exulted him, memorized his words, aped his attitudes,
swore allegiance to him, died for him, killed for him—
and he never told them a single thing they needed to hear:
Not ONCE did his words make one of his fans
look about and think, "Where am I? AM I? WHO
am I? What am I doing here and why?" And by the time
he told them they all deserved to die for failing him—
by that time that was what they WANTED to hear,
rather than face their failure, and he was insane
and led his nation and the world into insanity, huge piles
of broken bricks, bones, old shoes and women's hair
as a score of millions died— you think you can beat
that score? You think you can beat Hitler
in a poetry slam? Do you? What if he comes back without
that funny mustache? What if he's a skinny pimply kid
with sad, burning blue eyes and purple spiked hair?
What if he's black, Hispanic, a woman? What if he's got
a rich deep voice and a world of woe? What if he's got
a hearty laugh and perfect comic timing? Could you beat
Hitler in a poetry slam? How? By out-Hitlering him?
You gonna yell louder, whisper softer, exude
more toxic venom? You gonna hurt more and
hate better and find easier "solutions?" You gonna
pile the bodies higher? Maybe so— maybe you can
do that. But even if you can, that's
the EASY way to win a poetry slam.

                                                    Dean Blehert

Lest We Forget

Ronald Reagan is alive but forgetting things.
An elephant never forgets, but this is
personal, not political. We must make that distinction
or all our politicians would be institutionalized
for forgetting their promises.
Ronald Reagan is alive but forgetting things.
In his day he was called "Teflon" because
nothing stuck to him; now even memory
turns slippery.

Ronald Reagan is alive but forgetting things.
Nancy went to his birthday party without him.
Was he missed? Probably not–so many people
know how to "do" Ronald Reagan...

Ronald Reagan is alive but forgetting things.
What was it he said about the dead storm troopers?
That they, like those they killed, were victims?
Was that a remembering or a forgetting?

Ronald Reagan is alive but forgetting things.
He said Americans should be proud of being
American. Was that a remembering or a
forgetting?

Ronald Reagan is alive but forgetting things.
He used to know a great many things by rote–
that is, by heart, such as movie scripts, the
speech he took on tour–who knows how much
else he was or seemed to be was memorized,
is now forgotten or comes back only
in random bits?

Ronald Reagan is alive but forgetting things.
He's forgotten about sending arms to Iran
for hostages–if he ever knew. If he ever
knew, he's forgotten he knew. He does not
at this time recall. He may have been an
honest man. If not, he is becoming one.

Ronald Reagan is alive but forgetting things.
Nancy is taking good care of him. If he were

still President, probably we wouldn't be told.
Would we notice?

Ronald Reagan is alive but forgetting things.
He used to be a spokesman for General Electric:
"Progress is our most important product!"–can
you still say that? Come on...Progress? ...Progress?

Ronald Reagan is alive but forgetting things.
He is–has always been–such an easy target.
Now he's a sitting duck. It's not sporting to say
these things. He suffers from a disease. It could
happen to anyone. It could start at the top of
our nation and trickle down to the rest of us.

Ronald Reagan is alive but forgetting things.
It's not so bad: He can still play golf with
Hope. And now even his own children
speak well of him.

Ronald Reagan is alive but forgetting things.
He is loved and hated for wanting to shrink
government, for failing to shrink government,
for forgetting the poor, for remembering the
rich, etc. He is loathed and adored for saying
it is not evil for a person or nation to prosper
and be strong. Now here's the odd thing: Nearly
everyone hates or loves Ronald Reagan for something
he said or is said to have said, and everyone
is certain that somehow events have justified
this love or hatred, but hardly anyone remembers
(or ever knew) just what Reagan did or what
came of it or how much of what has happened since
came of it. Today's newspapers are already a gray
blur. Tell me, who are these candidates really?
Even our pain becomes unreal the moment our
President feels it. What is the difference
between such knowing and forgetting?

Ronald Reagan is alive but forgetting things.
He proved that an actor playing the role
of a political leader is impossible to
distinguish from a political leader. Is this
something we should remember or forget?

Ronald Reagan is alive but forgetting things.
His baiting the Evil Empire and his "Star Wars"plan
were so stupid that maybe they ended the cold war.
Lebanon, Libya, Grenada... His idiotic economics
brought us huge economic expansion–or was it
ruin? Or was that because of the liberal congress?
O Listen, I can't think with such stuff. I remember
only "Doonesbury" and that full forelock awaft on
helicopter wash that drowns out his smiling voice.

Ronald Reagan is alive but forgetting things.
Does he still have a full head of hair? Does
Nancy tint it? Does he stammer more now, quaver,
jowls shaking? Can he still grin that grin?
Is there anything he must forget to be able to grin
that grin? Is he cheerful about forgetting?
Can he joke about it? Isn't Ronald Reagan
a pretty nice guy? Nicer than Nixon, anyway?

Ronald Reagan is alive but forgetting things.
Even as we speak Ronald Reagan is forgetting
things. There is so MUCH to forget! He has
just this moment forgotten "where's the
rest of me?" and now he's forgotten preferring
to be in Philadelphia...and there goes "There
you go again!" But there is more–
so much more to forget.

Ronald Reagan is alive but forgetting things.
We, too, are alive but forgetting things.
"Surveys show that 60% of those under 18
don't know..."–that we fought in Vietnam,
that we didn't win in Vietnam, who Roosevelt
was or Truman or Ike (Does anyone remember
Gerald Ford?)–and one-year-olds have
forgotten almost everything, though some
have remembered how to grin that grin.

Ronald Reagan is alive but forgetting things.
And us? With each new miracle drug, we forget
all the earlier miracle drugs that are now
called evil drugs. We all know that things
have always been the way things are and so
must always be so.

Ronald Reagan is alive but forgetting things.
If we can forget fast enough, we will, at last,
be able to live in the eternal present, having
no past nor future—100% guilt-free,
without plans, budgets, debts or regrets.
Someone will take care of us—maybe the Government,
for hasn't the Government always taken care
of the People? Ronald Reagan, of course, preached
self-reliance, but Ronald Reagan probably
isn't allowed to go for a walk alone now
lest he get confused—all those Pacific Palisades
mansions look pretty much alike.

Ronald Reagan is alive but forgetting things.
Soon we will forget Ronald Reagan. It is said
that what we forget we must repeat. We will
forget Vietnam (he helped us) and have to do it
again. We will forget the Holocaust and have
to do it again. We will forget slavery and
have to do it again. We will forget religious
intolerance and racism and ignorance and greed
and cruelty and have to do them again. We will
forget ourselves and have to do them again.
We will even forget forgetting and have to
forget again. And so we will have to do
Ronald Reagan again. He will die and be forgotten,
but when we need him, once again Ronald Reagan
will be alive for us, forgetting things.

                                        Dean Blehert

Focus
   dedicated to the work of Robert Richter

The shape of the fruit is firm in my hand,
its yellow arc a grin turned frown.
The man who harvested my breakfast
may now be sterile, standing under a Costa Rican sun

stripped of what made him macho
by chemicals, my perceived need for photogenic, unblemished bananas.

27

I wish the telephone would ring, announce
one of those frequent opinion polls, the ones
that ask me questions I would never
seek to answer. I wish Carmen Miranda
would ring my doorbell, samba into my kitchen,
a pesticide-laced fruit salad on her head.
I'd have something to say:

Bruise the fruit please, not the handlers.
I can live without supermarket sheen, can
tolerate surface imperfections. I'll spoon
mashed pulp into my baby's first world
mouth and never need to imagine the click, click
vacation slide show of an anonymous woman
rocking - her arms, her womb, her man, empty,
under an Ektachrome sun.

Jennifer Ley

RAMON
politica de la frontera

Come, Ramon, before the lights go out & these wiry young men hoist
themselves over the wall to disappear beyond mesquite & sage, we can still
bend back a long-necked Corona, sit awhile & talk of times passed, of wives
& lovers come & gone. Here, Ramon,

before their ghosts steal your dreams stitched to razor-wire & shrouds, we
can offer ten hail Marias for your sister in El Paso, Pablo in Chicago,
Elaina, your first wife, in San Juan.

While there's still time, Ramon, harden their hands in buckets of brine,
make them run for hours in the sun, pump iron /while there's still time,
teach: "I will work. We need to sleep. Is there a doctor ?" Come, Ramon,

while your aunt waits for her pesos at the edge of town & your brother
tunes his ancient Dodge, we can walk though history again, remember your
abeula's tales of her father's fat ranchero in Old California / the lashing
your old man fought in San Diego / sweet revenge on Imperial Beach.
Ramon,

28

it's true, you whipped your sister for fucking that Marine from Mariposa,
cut a young recruit for his suit, smuggled skag & coke to Canada? Wait!

I mean no disrespect. Something's out of whack. How long before truth
rolls over grief? Buried deep. Deep as the fact of tortured nuns rotting in a
Guatemalan pit /as the carcass of your cousin stiffens & cracks in a desert
east of San Diego.

Here, Ramon, as the light closes down we must take our chance, spend this
hour without remorse, without venom, without ache. We've come this far.
We wont forget. Here, I grip your hand. You must do the same for me.

Roger Aplon

I Carry the Dead

I carry the dead child in my pack
with dried fish my canteen
& a sealed tin of plums.
I carry his bloody shirt in my belt
his favorite toy
a pup he'd had since birth
over my shoulder
its eyes jiggle & snap
its stuffing leaks
it knocks against my ribs with every step.

I raised this child from his mother's arms
washed his puckered skin
combed dust from his hair
picked crusted tears from under his eyes
pearls of shit that clung in strands to his stubby legs.

I bear this boy with a hunter's grace
careful to measure my stride
conserving breath
past men eating fire
past manicured lawns
past peddlers of teeth.

I take this stiff corpse
no more than one year old
to dig his grave beyond the trees
where his people grazed sheep
honed tools
married
under bows of flowers
where a stream may at any moment
break through polished stone.

Roger Aplon

My Song

My
song got broken
glass
in it
and a lot
of unpaid bills
and footprints
of rodents
and the stench
of piss
and the echos
of gunshots
and the snap
of broken necks
and the screams
of the terrified.

My song
cuts my
throat
with razor edged pain
of journeys
taken in bottoms
of ships.

My song
is filled
with the flames

of many fires
and the ashes
of many bones.

My song
is thrown spears
and speeding bullets
on missions
of glory.

Lamont Steptoe

527 Est 23rd St

Every other day
flashing lights arrive at your door
Every other day
red lights flash to collect
the red blood you're not allowed to touch
Every other day
a new occupant is welcome
Every other day
an old friend gets a ride
Every other day
I pray it's not you
Every other day
You don't cry
because you knew
Every other day
You welcome a new friend
say good bye to an old.
Every other day
You say
I'll show you to your room.

Cynthia McCallion

A Jew in New York

Like everybody else, I wasn't a Jew
Until I came to New York. In Portland, OR,
The other day, a young Latina asked me
If I were Jewyorican. Papa and Bubby
Came from Ukraine, landed in Brooklyn,
Settled in Harlan, KY, and named my father
Benjamin Franklin. My mother, the offspring
Of a coalminer, married Ben, the only Jew
In town. He didn't last. Ma remarried.
In kindergarten, in Cincinnati, instead
Of moving to the afternoon session the second

Semester, I stayed in Morning and changed my name.
This is the year 5755. In Chinese it is Year
of the Dog. I am 45 years old, and learned that the time between
Rosh Hashona (Jewish New Year) and Yom Kippur (Day
of Atonement) are the Days of Awe. Moody and gray,
with dashes of absolute clarity, I love these days.
Cleansing the summer's sweat from the streets of New York,
I always think of the Year beginning in September.
"That's when school starts." A holdover from Youth.
This year, 1994, for the first time I thought,
Hey, it's the real New Year, and I am a real Jew.
A real Jew, and a real coalminer's son, too.

Bob Holman

---

stinging

guess
that's how
it happens
you wake up one
morning
the light is
distant
and you are alone
cat dragging
something
past

the fridge
who will put the
flowers on
Joe DiMaggio's
grave
when the rain
is like ice
stinging
like a
bumble bee
tangled
in the trees
go ahead
the light is
green.

E. Gironda, Jr

Proof of Disorder

So that the blood spilled in Hastings
Puddles into pasty swells of dark sap,

And hen hardens into the Rorschach piecework
Of gleaned over fossils, rather than guess...

We offer you proof.
Proof our ancestral faces

Scaled these embattled walls
Burst into courtyard and settled

Her imperial colors with mace
And sword and shiv, sure to be heard,

"The manifest hour is near..."
Gods barren prize of crowned nipples

Wagers unaware in sleep
Still to be certain that the Viet Congs'

Troop markings, missile ledgers and shells
Of oxidized metals are fingerprint clear.

33

We offer you proof.
Evidence of hypnotic anthems,

Bright lights and bells and ceremony
That baptized parades underfoot.

In snippets of speech to be heard...,
"The manifest hour is near.."

Let Juris Prudence guide our united,
Indivisible, god-fearing, comrades
Through unethical terrains.
 Yet to be positive history's

Archives are bound, sealed
with the hand-twisted whipcords

And lashed into time's redress,
Rather than guess...We offer this proof.

David Hunter Sutherland

Whether we impeach the snow
or censure the frost
a cool change has hit
some are already frozen in their attitudes
some rain down opinions
others drizzle on about rules of law
but the weather won't be controlled
hurricanes of public opinions are gathering
Tsunami tidal waves of reactionary politics
drown us in unnatural deluge
and we shelter from the storm
while lightning strikes. twice
hitting, like all good music
the conductor
first.

Thom World Poet

Lancondon

What keeps you so?

You draw my heart to you with hooks, oh
Lancondon of selva. The last percent
of humanity that resists the Spanish fly
of Chiapas under thatched roofs and barking dogs... where first
there was laid that maggot
parasite of twisted Catholic processes,
still feeding on the wounds of their own creation. You were
scourged and mangled into oppression, but still remained resistant.
That island of pure Mayan blood, the last five hundred,
the soul of Chiapas, still sing to the jaguar song.
What keeps you so?

They thought your back was broken.
By the heat of white fever virus, by the heat
of countless deaths in the name of gold, by the heat of your burned
books, codices, and hopes, all for the exchange of dogmatic truths–and
what of the drug lord? Still you cling to what you find was never lost
inside.
What keeps you so?

Deep in la selva you drag your chains
to be heard. Your diamond patched frocks
over eagle motifs still cling to the great wheel
of your ancestors. Your long count calendar mark the days by cycles
of concentric spirals, repeating. You were connected with the past, a long
past, and a future they say ends in   2006...
Do you ring in the new age by example?
What keeps you so?

The rain forest echoes of La Ruta: of DDT
and Aids, of PEMEX trucks on mud rut roads,
of coffee, banana, sorghum, cocoa and
chicloros, tobacco, and the filtered jewels
of marijuana, and coke plantations;
of alcoholism and tuberculosis, malnutrition
and cattle carrying parasites.
Hachakyum, help you! "Tengo mi pistola, me mota, y mis huevos.
Entiendes mendez?
What keeps you so?

35

Trucha! Yo estoy hecha de otro arbol! Your hooks are deep
in my swelling heart... Hide, oh Lancondon. Hide in la selva!
Survive Zapatistas, and the Mexican Army. Hide from absorption,
hide from genocide!

Ken La Rive

Final Rain

After the final rain
Deer leaped & fell on their sides, looked for the hunters & their guns, saw
none, but saw the sun blotted out.Their eyes & nostrils filled with ash.They
kicked beneath the ash, then fell into themselves in a dream in which they
drank from cold streams & cropped the white flowered meadows.

After the final rain
Whales dove to escape the flaming oceans.They felt the pressure of the deep
increase, the harsh water rush into their mouths & lungs.Their bodies
collapsed: blood rose in a black cloud laced with red.

After the final rain
Horses jumped fences, fire for a rider, they galloped over smoking hills
toward a forest of charred logs.

After the final rain
The muskrat sat on its haunches, sniffed the wind, then tumbled
backwards,
The beaver ran from the burning woods to a lake that became a desert,
The wild dog bared its fangs and became a statue,
Herons streaked like firebrands into the secret swamp.

After the final rain
Rats fled all ships, all cities, & crowded the open fields where they ran,
fucked, fought, tore out the eyes, the hearts of dead goats & cows &
burned & burned
in a shrieking brigade.
Spiders touched their webs like harps of flame:
their music the collapse of bridges, the scream of jet engines.

After the final rain
That children should have played in until the first crack of thunder & their
mothers should have called: come in children, come in & dry off;
That fathers should have driven home in from a hard day at the factory,

their windshield wipers slicing the blear away;
That career women should have ridden
the train home in, falling asleep where they stood with their wrists hanging
like a swan's broken neck through the metal loop, the newspaper slowly
sliding from beneath their arms; That the maverick thinker for I.B.M.
walking through the park should have gotten the final theorem correct in,
& reached in his pocket for a drenched notepad & a stub of pencil;
That should have caused the old man with no teeth to wrap himself tighter
in newspapers in his home under the highway overpass, and the old
woman to pull a plastic trashbag over her stinking dress; That should have
driven the runaway girl into the arms of her pimp for the warmth she
thought she could find there, & the young boy with the run-down shoes for
his needle and his stained cotton; That should have collected in puddles for
snakes to lie in, and water striders to dart across between the unsettling
drops; That should have washed the birdshit from the tombs of the famous,
or watered the weeds on unmarked mounds; That should have drenched
the discarded charcoal portrait of a young woman, left crumbled in the
park by the artist who was not satisfied with the result,

the hard outline of the face softening, shadows beneath the chin becoming
more delicate with each rich drop; That should have ruined the freshly-cut
hay, driven the lovers indoors, drowned the domesticated turkeys who are
too stupid to look down when a thunderclap makes them raise their beaks
to the sky...

After the final rain
I hung my banjo in the charred branches of an oak, I ran my fingers
through my flaming hair, I called out the names of my friends, my sons,
the woman I thought I loved & leaned back between the red ribs of the sky
& the black ribs of the earth & Saw no god in the clouds with a human face
like mine ready to uncreate me, take back the breath so generously
bestowed
upon my clay...

       only
           one
      silver
            missile
          tumbled
          down.

                                     Jesse Glass

Incomplete Examination

Until I say–no, no more–the physician
specifically trained for such occasions,
examines me naked late the next afternoon,
inch by careful inch, slowly touching me slowly
everywhere slowly. You are ovulating, he says.
He has pills for that, among other things.
He remarks upon raw skin, bruises.
Keeps finding bruise after bruise. I can not connect
bruises with what happened and I can not talk any more.
Old, I say, fall down. I can not talk any more.
I have already talked with the center director,
the policewoman, the center director, the psychologist,
the center director. I can not talk any more.
Could I describe the rape for him, he says.
Minor, I say. Ordinary.

Frances Driscoll

A Season of Beens

   Y'know these wings, these
wings I own–been
     railed against & burned
  been tested too far

   Y'know this flight, this
flight been on–been
     shut down much-many times
  been run aground

  but Y'know this heart, this
heart much stood–been
     stilled in storm
  been strong to it all

  and Y'know this crown, this
sun that sits–been
     put for a spell for a season
  right there, been put underneath–
for a reason

Edwin Torres

The Box and Its Future Politics

There was a homemade wooden box, and in it
sets of children's battered alphabet blocks.
They often built a skyscraper with them,
   eight blocks to a floor,
and to separate the floors used thin books,
each of which told about an Indian tribe.
Their fingers weren't always clean,
and the pale wood blocks got brown fast.

They rolled toy cars against the building,
to see it crash over the floor, and each time
the blocks lost a splinter here, a little paint there.
They would open the scattered Indian structural elements
     and read about Indians.
     Their mother urged them,
and then demanded, with dinner time close,
that they put things where they belonged.

She could have said clean up that mess,
   they later realized.
She liked to ask, when they started,
what they were building this time,
as if it was supposed to be different.

So as they grew up they sort of understood
that your hands would get dirty,
   and so would what you touched.
And you could learn things in the ruins,
and people maybe smarter were maybe watching and hoping,
and play was play and work was work.

Play was people putting up something in somebody else's way,
whenever they felt like it, asking no leave,
     because they liked doing it.
Play was pretending that a tiny car
collapsing some structure in just two or three tries
was a cheerful approximation of reality.

Work was thinking about building something different,
   and better, and really doing it, all together.

                        Charles Vandersee

Teacup Politics

Little fingers pointed up,
we drink blindly
but in a mannerly fashion
from watered down, weakened tanic solutions.
Social and political teabags wrung
too many times
and used again.

Watered down by apathy, hate
and misinformation
we suck up gallons of newspaper pap,
and political lies, not missing the demise
of delicate, democratic, eggshell china structure.

Satisfied with simple, saccharin solutions,
promises of a gentler, kinder tea
and false chamomile chants.

Not seeing teacup
fissures or leaking liquids
of "new and improved " cups,
"so much better than our parents!"
we say, our hue and cry.
We continue this
teaparty in a room held dark
by our own beliefs
in squeezed out government grounds.

I hold the old red, white and blue teacup
of our Uncles up to the light
with anger and tears in my eyes
and wonder how anyone
can ever see it as whole again.

Claiborne Schley Walsh

The History of Revolutions

You slew Goliath and became ... his clone.
Dave, break that cycle–smite with your harp, not stone.

Peter Viereck

For the Ethiopian Jews
Passover, 1982

Brothers, sisters, what does it mean
that you are not with us?
that you have died of thirst
on an earth babbling with water?
that you have died of hunger
in a world greasy with animal flesh?
What does it mean that you have been eaten
by disease and neglect? that you have drunk
deeply at the well of brutality and murder?

What does it mean to you, *Enange Addissu*?
Four daughters! Or to you, *Yigzaw Melanu*,
whose sorrows are numbered in sons?
The ground will warm again, trees yield
their pomp of blossoms, but
Teshale Atsuha, your wife!
Tilahun Solomon, your daughters!
Tamino Yiskias, your mother!
Balanbaras Yizhak, your sons!

Sisters, brothers, I too am going blind
from gazing at the scorched children
of Ethiopia. My life has caught fire
from these names that ignite
Solomon Tzazu!
Wohuale Wogldu!
Astede Zeyssanu!
Sahlitu Termias!

Blood of my blood, your silence
drinks me

Falashas,
I will feed your names to my heart

Charles Fishman

The Horizontal Brigade

In the old days the horizontal brigade won every battle. They had weapons
causing death more exotic than cobra bites, but they never used them.
Their music, played while hiding behind anything horizontal (fallen oaks,
divans, abandoned carriages), was their strength: charmed horses would
offer their glittering manes as booty when so tantalized. Foxholes were their
dollhouses, and so they were lovingly guarded. It was only in emergencies
when they called up the reserves, the infamous ponies immune to gravity
that bombed the clubfoot tanks. Veteran drivers surrendered more out of
novelty than fear. Only once, at the Battle of the Twirling Mists, were they
known to use the ultimate weapons, the costumes that rendered them
vertical yet fierce. Today we are surprised that such men could have
existed. It's like imagining the Age of Reason, when bearded philosophers
died in gold bathtubs under the gaze of admiring disciples.

Maxine Chernoff

Old Photograph. The Retreat from Prague

It is the fifth year of the war, and she is three.
He father holds her, carefully,
like a valise full of her mother's bones.

James Owens

Curve
For Alice Stewart

Using the language of science
she showed us the steep curve
mysterious on the graph
pointing to casualties of a certain kind.
Only over time
did the idea come to her, hidden
under this curve early deaths
of another sort produced a different but
invisible curve
making it
one long slope of dying.
All this proceeded
in a now to be calculated way

after the first explosion
began the chain of events
diminishment, loss
collapse, cancer
the disappearance of
family, friends.
Genetics? She said.
The children
the ones born later?
Yes, but that
is another study.
Perhaps next time,
another lecture.
The consequences
grim as they are
sterling clear.
There to see in the numbers,
one might easily infer
the stories,
the telling
blank spaces.

Susan Griffin

On the Way Home

On the way home
all the restaurants will serve miso soup

On the way home
exotic notebook stores will blossom in small towns in Nevada

On the way home
Utah will be festooned w/mirth
Mormons will be dancing in the streets in gauzy chatchkas

On the way home
Everyone will leave the casinos and the slot machines & go outside
to stare at the beauty of the mountains, of the sky, of each other

On the way home
All the boys & girls in the secret desert bordellos

43

will have set up temples of free love adorned with mimosa
they will teach karma-mudra to joyful redneck ranchers
who have set all their cows free and now drink only amrita

On the way home
every café in Wyoming will be holding a potlatch
poverty will thus be abolished

On the way home
everyone we meet will try to read us a poem
invite us in for a story there being no news
but what travelers bring, all TV having died

On the way home
it will be easy to find pure water,
organic tomatoes friendly conversation
We'll give & receive delightful music &
blessings at every gas station
(all the gas will be free)

On the way home
all the truck drivers will drive politely
the traveling summer tourists will beam at their kids
our old Toyota will love going up mountain passes
openhearted & unsuspicious people & lizards
prairie dogs, wolves & magpies will sing together & picnic
at sunset beside the road

Everyone will get where they're going
Everyone will be peaceful
Everyone will like it when they get there

All obstacles smoothed
auspiciousness & pleasure
will sit like a raven dakini
on every roof

Diane di Prima

Another American Metaphor

The melting pot be damned.
Cement me a mosaic.
Hard tiles burned in the crucible
of the soul. Give the vivid
colors! Panther black, rose red,
sapphire blue, loam brown, sunflower
yellow and moonlight white. Hard
tiles burned in the crucible
of the soul made flesh made
defeat made spirit-rise that hewed

hope from the bones of this nation–
a realization of canyons rimmed
 in justice...
Brimmed in unbroken benevolence
where peals of fresh philosophies ferment.
Cement me a mosaic. Give the vivid. Let each

tile tell its story. Let each tale rise
and blend... alter the atmosphere,
like the round womb of music
expressed in the marvelous logic
of mathematics discovered in the realm

of dream. Yes. Give the vivid.
An individual colorful miracle
contributes to the collective work
 of art...

The melting pot be damned.

LaVerne Williams

Newt's Nukes

Those people over there are eating yogurt for breakfast
and they're carrying two bags of potted plants.
They're from California.

Those people over there look like they buy their clothes in K-Mart
(and they're not exactly blonde and blue-eyed.) They're thieves.

All waiters in coffee bars are gay.

That woman over there would cut off my dick in a minute.
(She's a lawyer)

That woman over there in a mini skirt
would cut off my dick in a minute.
She's a tease (and a whore).

That woman over there is a feminist. (She's a lawyer
in a mini skirt and she looks like Gloria Steinem.)

All feminists are whores.

(Gloria Steinem is a whore.)

New York Jews are too rich for their own good.

All New York Jews are no good.

New York is filled with immigrants, children of immigrants, feminists,
thieves, gay waiters, African-Americans,
Jews and cab drivers with no manners.

Cab drivers from New York are no good.

(New York is no good).

All women who were born in New York would cut off your dick
in a minute and do not deserve respect unless you can be sure
they were not born there and they love children.

All women who were born in New York are no good.
All Irish people from New York or Boston
are Catholic and drunks.

All Irish Catholics from New York or Boston
should not be allowed to party
in white middle-class neighborhoods
because they were not raised on the
traditional American values upon which this country was built.

All Irish Catholics from New York or Boston are un-American.

JFK was a fluke.

JFK should never have been allowed to become President
because he was Irish Catholic from Boston and a liberal,
bleeding-heart Democrat.

All Democrats are bleeding-heart liberals who are either
native New Yorkers, immigrants, children of immigrants, thieves,
African-Americans, Irish Catholics, gay waiters, Jews, artists,
writers (especially poets) and/or feminists in mini skirts.

All Democrats are no good.

All artists and writers (especially poets) should not be allowed
to party in white middle-class neighborhoods
because most of them today are Democrats.

All artists and writers (especially poets) are un-American.
(Walt Whitman was a fluke)

The Bible is the one true book.

All books (except for the Bible) should be burned.

Cynthia Andrews

Residencia En La Tierra

microcosm. macrocosm.
star. quasar.
steady state
the iguana expanding through time
walking out of the sea
onto the continent of South America
in the third year. inhaling the air
the humid seeping of time in the tropics.

steady state
through the years. the unraveling ball
the constant inhaling of air
all the stored up knowledge in the lung cells

of the first reptile
low flame
the sun's intoxicating
time is a delicate drug in Ecuador.
lazy. lack of movement. sun spots.
every other century a vessel bursting
depris. cracks. faults in the land.
Peru is wracked with earthquakes
restless shifting
the great bang explosion of the Andes overnight
catastrophic

a mere split on the side of iguana
a jolt to his grip. his gears
his procession over the continent
pulling his belly along the ground
he wants to make love
they eat him like chicken. split him in two
matter reduces to matter
the rains are strange in the Amazon. river of reptiles

Janet Hamill

I Believe

They dragged him by his ankles
chained to the back of their truck
strewing flesh and limbs
across a blood-stained two-mile stretch of Texas road
 as the New York Post ran yet another picture
 of Monica Lewinsky on its front cover
 and you ask why I don't believe in God?

I believe in humanity's infinite capacity
 for good and evil.
I believe that all men are created equal.
I believe there is nothing more divisive
 than the concept of a chosen people.

The ignorance of an individual
is representative of nothing
    but that individual's ignorance.

48

The persistence of stereotypes
makes every black man a nigger
      every white man a devil
but linear thinking leads to illogical lives
promoting racial divides
with whites hating blacks hating browns
forgetting the reds were here first
while the yellows fly under the racial radar
    because everybody thinks it's okay to hate them.

If I believed in God
I'd pray for another flood
to cover the earth in thick, brown mud
and any survivors would be covered in it, too
thick, brown and impenetrable
like the earth herself
    united in tragedy   starting over from scratch.

But I don't believe in that.

I believe, if there ever was a God
    He's moved on
      a disappointed parent who decided his children were grown
    and would not change
and my soul dies a little more each day.

I believe James Byrd Jr.
 died a death too horrible for metaphors
as humanity took one more step
   towards the abyss.

                                 Guy LeCharles Gonzalez

Another Nameless Prostitute
Says the Man Is Innocent
–for Mumia Abu-Jamal
–Philadelphia, PA/Camden, NJ, April 1997

The Board-blinded windows knew what happened;
the pavement sleepers of Philadelphia, groaning
in their ghost-infested sleep, knew what happened;
every black man blessed
with the gashed eyebrow of nightsticks
knew what happened;
even Walt Whitman knew what happened,
poet a century dead, keeping vigil
from the tomb on the other side of the bridge.

More than fifteen years ago,
the cataract stare of the cruiser's headlights,
the impossible angle of the bullet,
the tributaries and lakes of blood,
Officer Faulkner dead, suspect Mumia shot in the chest,
the witnesses who saw a gunman
running away, his heart and feet thudding.

The nameless prostitutes know,
hunched at the curb, their bare legs chilled.
Their faces squinted to see that night,
rouged with faded bruises. Now the faces fade.
Perhaps an eyewitness putrefies eyes open in a bed of soil,
or floats in the warm gulf stream of her addiction,
or hides from the fanged whispers of the police
in the tomb of Walt Whitman,
where the granite door is open
and fugitive slaves may rest.

Mumia: the Panther beret, the thinking dreadlocks,
dissident words that swarmed the microphone like a hive,
sharing meals with people named Africa,
calling out their names even after the police bombardment
that charred their black bodies.
So the governor has signed the death warrant.
The executioner's needle would flush the poison
down into Mumia's writing hand
so the fingers curl like a burned spider;

his calm questioning mouth would grow numb,
and everywhere radios sputter to silence, in his memory.

The veiled prostitutes are gone,
gone to the segregated balcony of whores.
But the newspaper reports that another nameless prostitute
says the man is innocent, that she will testify at the next hearing.
Beyond the courthouse, a multitude of witnesses chants, prays,
shouts for his prison to collapse, a shack in a hurricane.

Mumia, if the last nameless prostitute
becomes an unraveling turban of steam,
if the judges' robes become clouds of ink
swirling like octopus deception,
if the shroud becomes your Amish quilt,
if your dreadlocks are snipped during autopsy,

then drift above the ruined RCA factory
that once birthed radios
to the tomb of Walt Whitman,
where the granite door is open
and fugitive slaves may rest.

Martín Espada

For the Jim Crow Mexican Restaurant
in Cambridge, Massachusetts Where My Cousin
Esteban Was Forbidden to Wait Tables
Because He Wears Dreadlocks

I have noticed that the hostess in peasant dress,
the wait staff and the boss
share the complexion of a flour tortilla.
I have spooked the servers at my table
by trilling the word burrito.
I am aware of your T-shirt solidarity
with the refugees of the Américas,
since they steam in your kitchen.
I know my cousin Esteban the sculptor
rolled tortillas in your kitchen with the fingertips
of ancestral Puerto Rican cigarmakers.
I understand he wanted to be a waiter,

but you proclaimed his black dreadlocks unclean,
so he hissed in Spanish
and his apron collapsed on the floor.

May La Migra handcuff the wait staff
as suspected illegal aliens from Canada;
may a hundred mice dive from the oven
like diminutive leaping dolphins
during your board of Health inspection;
may the kitchen workers strike, sitting
with folded hands as enchiladas blacken
and twisters of smoke panic the customers;
may a Zapatista squadron commandeer the refrigerator,
liberating a pillar of tortillas at gunpoint;
may you hallucinate dreadlocks
braided in thick vines around your ankles;
and may the Aztec gods pinned like butterflies
to the menu wait for you in the parking lot
at midnight, demanding that you spell their names.

Martin Espada

===

Lafayette Park, Morning after Impeachment

Lafayette Park,
morning after impeachment,

the homeless men stroll past
the latest curios--

hand-painted wooden dolls of the
president's known infidelities.

On a bench
one man sits
facing the
White House

indifferent to approval polls,
sudden resignations,

constitutional standards,
doctrines of global reality,

eloquent arguments made
                in the national spotlight,

                        reading the news
                        in someone's
                        discarded
                        Sunday paper.

Jim Cohn

===

Ravages

An oil fire down below, and on the lit box
an unmoving figure, a man from behind, forearms
bare, walking a path that curves through cared for
green, each plant placed so unfurling it sculpts
a sort of speech. I breathe with difficulty
and darkness rises from the snow. All month
I've been precarious, at a threshold, near
an entrance. No one will say what lies
or what tells the truth. No one can.
If I could, for once, make another visible
this way – outside cars slice silent air,
and they say the weather's changing.
Last night I heard a man last night declare with pride
he no longer reads the news – and what they do
they do in our name. Yes, she is beautiful,
like a wide river or an uncomplicated view
of the ocean, but my eyes blank – even
inner vision can't see her now. Such a wide
silence suddenly I've lost my taste
for spiritual ventriloquy, want to know
just the circling of my own pale hours.
How did this happen again? Nothing happens
again. Eccentricity in her walk, a tilt
as she moves, and I watch as the taxi pulls
south, as she diminished, the driver's language
nothing I can speak. Every time she's left,
I've let her go without protest, and as
the print of her body leaves mine, ceased
to understand myself. Shoppers interrupted
crossing a street; at the next cut, faces
turned to the wall, blood splashed up stucco;

then the look of wound-scraped skin,
a dying face in bright color. I stay away
from the news, he says. Frozen rain picks at
window glass and illness sinks through my abdomen.
I'd get an image of your face and long to
fall toward you into touch, just touch.
A desert, the sickle moon, a black sky
and fire lights her face. Here, light seems to
crack not extend, and I can't remember
who died yesterday. He was not
old, and he did what I do at the desk,
something beneath his hands to put word to paper.
As we stood there, she pulled me toward her
by the belt and thrust in with her hand.
Tonight cold divides skin from body heat.
What was it like before cars? before oil burned
in the cellar or jets blanched the sky as if
speed made a difference? In a sunlit room,
I love you more... In the kitchen, orange
clivia, its yellow centers, how its broad leaves
shape the light. If I followed her, would I turn
to look back? We're through half our lives.
Yes, I answer, as if there were no dead
on certain streets in Europe, no shoppers
hurrying across a square as a wall shudders
from the end of a room – and through a window
you see a face dart forward. On waking,
I beg in the empty dark. Was this a life?
It's the same magenta comforter my sister
carried from Norway as I lay in an oak bed
with a man who loved me, before the telephone
kept memory or screens were linked to language.
It's as if I missed ten or twenty years, certain
lengths of skirt, cuts of jacket. That's where
the Chinese Laundry was! I remember the day
I went to say goodbye, the man looking at me
with a fast smile. I was sure I was going somewhere.
Here, from below the fields late at night,
you can hear the train along the river wailing,
wailing hard, between water and the mountains.

Honor Moore

Port Royal

I THE FISHERMEN

Jamaica, 1960

Ignoring the local reliquiae
—neoclassical arches in ruin,
courtyards, their fountains toppled,

prados flourishing in prickle-weed, esplanades
no longer level enough to collect rainwater,
much less respect for the *Imperio de España*

tarnished by an islander's mock-British accent—
two fishermen returned at sundown.
Antiquaries themselves, these fishermen

schooled in the currents, the tide,
the tunneled limestone of the coral reefs,
preferred the graceful curves of the £.

At the landing, five children, single file,
marched away the birds like soldiers,
the learned lyrics escaping their lips:

Rule Britannia, Britannia rules the waves.

II QUEEN'S SAPPHIRES

December, 1992

Here, Rome falls again and again—
the wind whistling a classic

through arches that can only feign decay
when compared to their Spanish cousins.

Once again, I have returned
to pace the crumbling sidewalks,

Port Royal the only remnant of Spain
on an island too devoted to the British.

Anxiety of crotons ripping up the esplanades,
sadness of palms leaning toward the sea . . .

On every column, the determination of vines
to honor the jewels of a dead Spanish queen

with flowers as blue as blood.

C. Dale Young

═══

Blues on Yellow

The canary died in the gold mine, her dreams got lost in the sieve.
The canary died in the gold mine, her dreams got lost in the sieve.
Her husband the crow killed under the railroad,
   the spokes dost shorn his wings.

Something's cookin' in Chin's kitchen,
   ten thousand yellow bellied sap suckers baked in a pie.
Something's cookin' in Chin's kitchen,
   ten thousand yellow bellied sap suckers baked in a pie.
Something's cookin' in Chin's kitchen, die die yellow bird, die die.

O crack an egg on the griddle, yellow will ooze into white.
O crack an egg on the griddle, yellow will ooze into white.
Run, run, sweet little Puritan, yellow will ooze into white.

If you cut my yellow wrists, I'll teach my toes to write.
If you cut my yellow wrists, I'll teach my toes to write.
If you cut my yellow fists, I'll teach my yellow feet to fight.

Do not be afraid to perish, my mother,
   Buddha's compassion is nigh.
Do not be afraid to perish, my mother,
   our boats will sail tonight.
Your babies will reach the promiseland,
   the stars will be their guide.

I am so mellow yellow, mellow yellow, Buddha sings in my veins.
I am so mellow yellow, mellow yellow, Buddha sings in my veins.
O take me to the land of the unreborn, there's no life on earth
   Without pain.

Marilyn Chin

time enough

the second the world ends,
prostitute Sadhana Mukherjee
will be standing with a woman
in a pastel sari
in a Calcuttan alley. She will be
speaking of condoms and unions,
of health and the power of walking
away.

the instant the world ends,
I will be
plucking my eyebrows
or salting slugs
in the garden.

Marty McConnell

Politics as Usual
To Syavesh, et al.

You tell me
I am not political
that my poems have no meaning
to any outside
those who have shared the experience.

when every time
I open my legs
politics comes to bed.

when any poem
of politics I write
would still be relegated
to the Women's Studies section
of the bookstore.

...because Hysteria comes from the Greek word for uterus.

AND I'm just a slut because I told you NO NO NO and you wouldn't stop
     but I was paralyzed after all weren't you a nice guy? And my
     judgement couldn't be off because wasn't I too intuitive for that?

SO when I just blew you to make you go away and my mouth tasted like I
        had eaten gravel for days and why did I feel so guilty? And I had
        to run to run to another boy for him to absolve me and he taught
        me how to defend myself.

AND aren't I one of the smart ones?

BUT when he told me I was too fat to sleep with.
AND when a 'poet' said a girl was "pretty enough to fuck."
AND when they look at me and assume I'm stupid.
AND when my friend used to have to cover her bruises on her arms.
AND half my friends have been raped.
AND I haven't been able to date anyone in two years because I just figured
        out who I am and I like her I like her. Please don't go away.

And I wonder –

Is there no country
I can escape to
to claim political asylum
from being female?

                                                        Kyrce Swenson

Somewhere Along The Line

What interested me most about gorillas
        when I first studied them
Was not that the males' penises are only
        two inches long,
But that gorillas shit and piss in their beds
        and don't leave to relieve themselves
                (though they build new beds every day),
Also they eat their feces, yes
        they eat their turds.
And this made me realize that we
        (somewhere along the line)
Decided we wouldn't shit and piss in our beds,
We agreed we wouldn't eat our shit
        or drink our piss,

That we would wear clothes
      and not go naked in public
            and not shit or piss in public
      and not jack off in public,
Not fuck or suck in public,
Not stick our fingers up our rear ends
      and smell them
            (even in the privacy
      of our own homes),
Or on meeting another of our kind
      sniff each other's cock and balls
            and cunt and asshole like a dog
      but shake hands like a man
And rather than pissing and shitting to mark
      our territory
We invented money
And rather than gathering food from plants
      we'd work to plant them raise them sell them
And rather than killing animals fish birds
      with our mouths and eating them
            raw and bloody
We'd hire others of our kind
      to kill them
            and cut them up into little pieces
      not with their mouths
            but with sharp knives in their hands,
And somewhere we decided rather than live in trees
      we'd kill them, cut them up into long pieces,
            build houses and live
      inside them while sitting in chairs
            made from them and write poems
      about them on paper made from them
            with a pencil made from them
      about how somewhere along the line
            we decided to be different than
      gorillas and monkeys because
            our way of being was right
      because we were better
            than any other creature on Earth.

                                                      Antler

Armageddon vs. Blowjobgeddon

I am a prophet of Blowjobgeddon!
Armageddon has been worshiped enough!!
"It's a boy." Code words
    to Truman
    that the A-bomb
    successfully dropped
    on Hiroshima.
That's the kind of boy
    military-industrialism desires.
That's the kind of ultimate orgasm
    capitalism results in.
The Four Blowjobs of the Apocalypse
    gallop to the rescue.
If you were a 15-year-old boy
    how would you rather have
    your Bible end–
With the destruction of the world
    or a deluxe blowjob?!

                      Antler

Chiapas 45

Chiapas 45
Chiapas 45
Chiapas 45

I am the oppressor and the oppressed
 but dont ever call me repressor or repressed because
  I believe in speaking freely and do so.

I am the oppressor and the oppressed
living in a crazy mixed up stone soup of poverty and affluence.
I have things that I dont need which is the definition of filthy rich,
yet most of my clothes are hand-me-downs
yet the furniture I sit on has been handed DOWn

I am the oppressor and the oppressed
I see so many folks around me without the things they need to be
H-A-P-P-Y (And I hear their babies cry for want)
I leave worn clothes and applied appliances and

played-with toys on the sidewalk and think that I am doing my part.

I spent a day among normal folks recently and
realized I no longer speak their language and
   they seem to me like filler, or fog,
like that styrofoam popcorn inside the great cardboard box of the earth

Weve got a 14 million dollar fence I see no need for borders
Mr. styrofoam-popcorn-soul America got a 14 million dollar fence!
The poets and the peace activists got one too
Until we dig a hole, or provide a safe house
for the weary we have got it too

Im not afraid to lose the little bit I have! yet
regret that I don't have the juevos
to be the good coyote in the new
underground railroad
bringing the slaves of circumstance to the pursuit of happiness
I am the oppressor and the oppressed
I stuff my face at the buffet // I dont leave a big mess for the busboy
I sleep comfortably in hotel beds // I clean up for the maid
I spend all day lollygagging on the fresh cut grass // I know who cut it

I drink until I get drunk // I cannot rationalize that
I fuck shit up // because shit needs to be fucked up.

Jimmy Jazz

Sky During a Time of War

Acres, and at the far edge
of the visible, a plowed field.
Prairie, golden, all the north
pouring cold through the elms.

           People
have left this place, leaving it
fertile, empty. Even high above
the curds of color, in the bare blue, there is
thin cloud, the layered landscapes
lifting above the flat, burned

stretch of pasture.
The bursts of pastel poise
between what has happened and what will be,
and the blank earth is unfinished under
the roll of rain. Somewhere
else, somewhere as full of taste as this

hard air so much
is open to fire. The other
side of the world: the phrase
on the tongue. This is
the emptiness inside things,

the gale through the syllables
of hope. Harvest is done,
and it is not enough.
Peace, but the cups
are nearly empty. Prayer,
but the words are chaff.

    This season
between tides suspends,
nowhere, mastering each
road. It goes on,
the iron falling from the blue.
Every home is air.

            Michael Cadnum

Graffiti

My children learn to read
with words like, "Fuck you,"
and "shit." They sound out

these words in alleys
on their way to school.

Words that Webster won't acknowledge
and their teachers won't allow.

My free lunch kids climb fences
in brickyards

where blue lights fill out forms
but don't bother to investigate.

My kids, can't spell 'cat' or 'dog,'
but spray paint their spite
on low income walls.
Their school pictures look
like mug shots.

They don't cry out for me
in the dark , because here,
"Mother" is just an abbreviation.

Carol Case

Bestiary

We are so many creatures—
dog-like devotion
and cat-like
independence;
sheep following
and wolf hunting.
We seek the calm
of cows,
grazing the richness,
patient and content.
Eagles and hawks,
at times,
flying
beyond tomorrow;
little mice,
seeking safety
in the grass.
We call ourselves
their masters,
confusing
in our pride,
the keeper
and the zoo

Terri Rolan

Arithmetic

The skyscraper crumbles to its knees,
its usefulness outworn, one supposes.
It has not kept up with its neighboring
financial district populated by
monumental highrises, landmarks
pointing the way to a bullish market
and a remote god even the local
New Jerusalem Tabernacle
has abandoned in favor of a more
accessible, indwelling Savior.

The man limping past the bus stop,
his green backpack a moving violation,
overspilling as it is with beer cans,
hunting knife, and half-chewed books,
is non-plussed by the building's demolition.
*No different than Korea of Nam. Another landmine
detonated, a corresponding grenade igniting
the interior of his skull. That platoon? How many lost?*
Numbers on storefronts and street signs
tilt into recitations of grade school counting lessons.

These days he is oblivious to sights, sounds,
downed electrical lines, onrushing traffic.
You name it. Everything that is, but smells.
The scent of anything rotting, half-eaten tacos
blackening fruit, squirrel intestines,
sends his right index finger
twitching as a barometer of disaster.
He licks the tip and holds it up to a derelict breeze.
If the wind is blowing from the east and his finger dries
quickly, he lowers his head, hunches his shoulders,
pushes past pedestrians, and squats
beside the nearest bench.

A tattered, outdated book slides
from its pouch, and a soiled medic's patch
stiffens the margin of the page delineating
the multiple cures derived from the application
of leeches to bare skin. As if in a trance,
he coaxes the knife free of its sheath
and carves another notch in his left forearm.

He is concentrating really hard.
He is in math class. Beads of sweat ring his eyes.
His head pivots and cocks backwards.
Blood criss-crosses the hatched surface,
coagulates into warm droplets he touches
reverentially. *That makes twelve.*

Caldor Lowe

Border Town

A border town lives always on the edge,
teetering on a man-made boundary
filled with GAWD and moonshine.
The moon is larger
and sings over a border town,
and all the border town people
know how to harmonize, dissonance
and minor key are our specialty.
Dance halls girls and miners
were our mothers and fathers
and nothing in a border town is
ever in the middle. It is a place
of extremes and only the lonely.
It is a very thirsty town and music
fills the night, even after local
honky tonks have closed, it wails
to the sound of the coal trains
passing empty, passing full,
as the black blood is drained
from the earth leaving -
the EPA to dig up every yard 6 inches deep,
paint it with blue seed
which cries in the rain blue tears
across the brick sidewalks
and into the cracks where
all the grass will grow.
Arkansas, Kansas, Oklahoma and Missouri
are just a swift run in any direction
and the people float back and forth
not knowing the CDC has marked them
one of the top ten cancer hot spots
in the U.S. of A.

We are famous, we are watched,
we are counted and studied
to predict the demise of those more
fortunate, we are the experimental file,
the chemo, radiation, cobalt,
CT scan, MRI gold mine.
Here in border town,
we only live in extremes,
always on the edge,
teetering on a man-made boundary
filled with GAWD and moonshine.

Pamela Postai

Puppet

Give me a string
and I'll sculpt your noose

before frayed ends navigate
through my course skin

wrapping limbs
entwining organs

before my bones take on
the formula for wood

because geppetto was not my creator

I learned responsibility
in a 17th century tavern cafe
serving coffee to yuppies
13 years old
I was paid under minimum wage
for 5 years

Read about humility
in concordances of war stories
the words leading refugee slaves
from barracks of the Ottoman soldiers
A ballad for independence beating in their ears
I'm free

they've set
me free
A diamond placed into battered eyes
snatched back by one holding a machete
stood behind the guards gate
and watched bloody necks roll
took bets on how far the headless torsos would run

Then saw schematics for underground governments
while strolling into a Manhattan bookstore
and seeing that the anarchy section
happened to be alphabetized

Heard segments of spiritual endarkment confined
for holy ghost belltones
inbetween Poe preaching to me
"The Lord is my rock and I smoke him"

and every stanza break
taught me to make
NOISE
felt for the dials

to find adjustment
in your diverse climates

YOU, MAN POLITICIAN FATHER

searching for the controls
that red button
Dickinson holds delicate
in her chest

YOU, MAN POLITICIAN FATHER

may believe that marionette
is embroidered against
your left breast
but
her open door policies
they control you
they
control you.

Amy Ouzoonian

She Won't Say She's Unhappy

Sometimes women don't lose
Their wedding bands
While doing the dishes.

Amy Ouzoonian

Bombs away over L. A.

We huddled around
Our respective coffees
Café au le
Cappuccino
Café late'
Designer fate out of our hands
Our eyes sublime
Drinking in the
Redundant Los Angeles sunshine
The news reflected from the paper
Was anything but good
The President of these United States
Was being called to task
By An International
Human
Rights
Tribunal
The mayor of Los Angeles
Was being called to task
By An International
Human
Rights
Tribunal
Undocumented sources
Reliable witnesses
Paid informants
Served notice on
Respective majesties
Reported crimes
In Technicolor
Hollywood noir
To United Nations
To Amnesties International

68

To The World Press
To Rupert Murdock
To Mickey Mouse himself
They were reliable
Dependable
Trustworthy
Almost desirable
Eyewitnesses to
Witting ruthlessness
As performed by the laidback Gestapo
Of the LAPD
On a consistent basis
Of hapless minorities
That had grown majority
And only blue suits kept their vision abated
Only blue suits kept the populace subdued
Rounding up their dreams
And prosecuting their nightmares
To the fullest extent of the law
Building citadel prisons
With dungeon precision
To incarcerate
To alienate
To eliminate
The so-called criminal element
In cries of three strikes you're out
Keeping their visions under lock and key
Imprisoned in the fortress of ineptitude
Solitary confinement for imagination
But the world was no longer
Looking the other way
Their faces turned to L.A.
Telling the mayor to toe the mark
Telling the president to not cross the line
But they pledged sovereignty
Not idle chatter
The United States of America
Was given deadline to cease and desist
The laurel wreathes of peace extended for the moment
But President and Mayor joining hands in sovereign promise
Refused with utter contempt to change ways
Homegrown and rooted in tradition
The United Nations under the direction of the Security Council
Canceling vetoes of its members

Declared Los Angeles fair game
To peace keeping Bombers
Tinsel town under attack
Shouted headlines in black and sharp white
Parker Center was ground zero
Bombs away over L.A.
Tell me it ain't so Mickey
Tell me it ain't so Donald
Goofy
Pluto
Popeye
Where are you when we need you
It's all illusion anyway
It's just another movie
Another cartoon comedy
Another siren goes off
Its air raid not cops
Bombs rain down on L.A.
The last headline spoke
Out of the blue
And the haze of Los Angeles sunshine
We are a sovereign nation
The President said
This is L.A. the Mayor said
City Hall destroyed the headline read
We are selecting only military targets
The combined forces reported
Paramount studios is forever in reruns
Sony is only a digital memory
The lion is gone from MGM
Universal is just another ride in their theme park
Disney is Mickey Mouse
Tinsel town detinselized...
The center of evil has been destroyed the BBC shouted!
The center of evil destroyed the BBC shouted!

Larry Jaffe

70

Solution to War

We should send old men and old women
to war, let them kill themselves off
in the name of bigger cars and better air-conditioning.

Let the congressmen and the presidents
pull out guns and knives and battle
rather than my son or my daughter.
Why should they fight for you
you fucking cocksuckers, you cowards.

You hide behind your hallow halls,
you hide behind the laws your money buys.

i want you out in the open
looking into a gun's barrel,
see what my son would see
before he pulled the trigger:
a man just like himself,
scared just like himself,
put there just like himself
by a man like you.

The blood should be yours mr president.
the guts spread on the ground
like used clothing at a fleamarket
should be yours speaker of the house.
the brains that splatter
Jackson Pollock studio rejects
should be yours senator.
Let our teenagers study math.
Let them tear down an engine
or hitchhike through europe
while they still have the balls
to protest your bullshit wars

Mikel K

When we passed the bus stop

at Missenden Road tonight
There was a man at the bus stop
"He's still there" the bus driver said.
It doesn't look like he's breathing.
He was curled up on the bitumen
with his arms crossed tight on his chest and his legs drawn up.
There was a pack of cigarettes and a box of matches
laid neatly on the seat.
The metho bottle was standing on the ground.
We'll soon find out, the bus driver said and
climbed down from the bus.
She bent over the man and touched him
lightly on the arm. The upper arm.
He did not move and she touched him again
feather gentle. He stirred, rocking back and forth,
his arms still clasped.
He's still breathing the bus driver said and
climbed back into the bus. He's still
breathing. And we drove away.

Michele Morgan

Would Jesus Die for a Monkey?

Would Jesus die for a monkey? Would Jesus die for a Martian? If Jesus lived, and Jesus died, and in doing so, changed the story for humans, then you are forced to face the question. Would He die for a monkey; would He die for a Martian?

Everyone who is awake must face the possibility that there is life beyond this planet. And every church worthy of the name acknowledges the possibility that human life is evolved from monkeys. Does Jesus care about Monkey life, and Martian life, and would he die for them?

I'm going to give you the orthodox Christian teaching on the matter, and then, of course, you may draw your own conclusions. But, when the topic comes up, as it surely must, your opinion will have an ascendant validity due to your ability to make reference to prevailing orthodox opinion on the matter.

Here it is, what one must believe to be fully in communion with any fully Christian church. I offer you all this information as a public service to do with as you will:

Jesus would not die for a monkey. He might die for a Martian.

Here is why: A monkey cannot need Jesus to die for him. If a monkey could have such a need, then Jesus would surely take the matter under advisement, give some thought to crawling up on a monkey cross to redeem all monkeydom. But a monkey can have no such need. A monkey is not capable of choosing to do that which it believes it ought not to do, THAT WHICH IT BELIEVES, BY IT'S OWN MONKEY STANDARDS, IT OUGHT NOT TO DO. Monkeys simply do what monkeys do. They respond to whichever stimuli is strongest. They do not have battles within their consciences, wherein they reach a determination of what they believe bo ne right, and then choose to do the opposite. If they did make such choices, Jesus might have to take on a monkey form and climb upon that monkey cross.

Now a Martian is a trickier question. It is possible to conceive of a Martian that reached a decision about what it ought to do, by its own Martian standards, and then chose to do the opposite. This is the predicament in which we humans find ourselves. We examine our consciences, and determine what we ought to do by our very own standards, and then willfully fail to do it. We know that a monkey can face no such dilemma, but we do not know that about Martians. If there were Martians consumed by remorse over their failures to be the sort of Martians they wished to be, if there were Martians burdened down to the point of emotional paralysis with the prices of their choices, and, for all we know, such may be the case, then Jesus would certainly be driven by compassion to put on tentacles and gills, myriad eyes and every nuance of Martian form, save for their foolhardy stubbornness, and climb up on a Martian cross for them.

And so consider, you children of monkeys, Jesus would not die for a monkey. Consider, you citizens of earth, of sun, of milky way, swirling, with innumerable galaxies swirling, through the inconceivable expanses of space, consider that Jesus might, or might not die for a Martian.

And know, each and every one of you, members of this absurd, sublime and bewildered race we call human, that Jesus would, and did, and would again if it would do us any good, die, for you, and for me.

Dave Sloan

73

...in 1875 it was testified in congress that the way to handle the Indian "problem" was to kill the buffalo. At the time there were about 65 million buffalo roaming the mid-western plains. Ten years later, only 150 head of buffalo could be accounted for. Early in 1997, buffalo once again were overpopulating Yellowstone National Park. The authorities decided to once again kill the buffalo. Interesting... the saga continues...

The Future of America in the belly of the beast

I am several nuances ahead of your green god
Good Lord, the radio says
they're still killing the buffalo
 still killing the buffalo
What will the Washington Redskins do now?

 now that the FBI has
killed
 Tupac and Biggie Smalls
Yes the FBI killed Tupac Shakur and Biggie Smalls
Yes the FBI
   Yes the FBI
Yes Fuckin' Bitchass Immigrant
from off the Mayflower honkeys killed Biggie Smalls
 Do you still think me exotic?
Would you rather I now wax erotic?
feel a lock thick with sweat
 whip thick and wet across your nipples
while the ripples of broken gov't contracts with the
Sioux and the newly freed niggaz
 still shatter South Bronx window panes
   and howl across
   barren reservation plains

O Shit!!!
 They're still killing the buffalo!

Have you seen the Aztec statues, luv?

 the lips the foreheads the eyes the cocks
 the Africans standing exalted on
South American plains a thousand years
 before the Middle Passage?

74

Now
we sell crack rock to your crack pot children
you say
 that's a crime

Amiri Baraka is the brightest most dynamic literary
figure of our age
and that brother still
had to change his name three times
 before
he knew he had found the spirit
 of his history.

That!!!

 Is a muthafuckin' crime
John 3:16
 For God so loved the world
 that He gave His only begotten son...
and we have killed in his name ever since
 and I'm not turning you on anymore, am I?

I am standing before you naked
sweat dripping off me
 limb by striated limb
 flowing from muscle to sinew to skin
to pool as a thick and salty
tidal wave at your feet
 But you'd rather I speak of
condors and the passion of wild animals
 Hell, they're still killing the buffalo
 They are still killing the buffalo.

You are flowing the richness
 of the four great herds
 before you -
You were born of and
nourished in their blood
 and retribution has
sliced your heart with your lying promises
to the Lakota and the Absarokee
/ we will dance
 the Ghost Dance on your heads
The wrath of Chango is coming!

America is full of beautiful people
america is full of beautiful people
and I still tremble
under the yoke of their smiles
and I do 200 push-ups a day in their honor
and masturbate to break beats with their names like gangsta rap
on my lips
 The web beams 3-D images
to South Dakota reservations
  and Brownsville projects
and cyberporn is more American than apple pie
 so if the breakdown of social barriers
is the legacy
of the war of independence
 Why are the Seminoles still in Florida?
  Why are the Seminoles still in Florida?
   Why are the Seminoles still in Florida?
and America's breadbasket now baking
 up more Timothy McVeighs armed
with Russian Aks
while we're raiding basements in Crown Heights for weapons
 preaching amnesty
 for niggaz
who were never really free.

My country 'tis of thee
 home of the muthafuckin' free
 land of the brave
everlasting domain of a nigga slave.

It is the year 2000 and I'm still
 "not quite cut out"
 for Wall Street employment
still
 "not quite ready"
 for country club enjoyment

and I'll moan your name when I cum

 but they're still killing the buffalo
  They're still killing the buffalo
    They are still killing the buffalo.

                              Roger Bonair-Agard

Speak Out

Anyone can say they're a Vietnam veteran. Anyone can say, "I did two, three tours in Vietnam, I was a medic, humped the boonies, got shot at, plugged guys with bandages and morphine to ease the pain." Anyone can say, "When I came back they dissed me, treated me like shit, but I ain't no whiner, I'm a genuine hero."

But not me. I'd never do that. I'm the real McCoy. The genuine article. The real deal. I served six thousand combat tours in Vietnam. I have the paperwork and medals to prove it.

At a warehouse in Secaucus, New Jersey, surrounded by electrified chain link fence, armed guards with six legged pit bulls who speak in tongues watch over my one hundred and eighty thousand Medals of Honor. On Tuesdays I charge $5.00 for the Radical Walking Tour.

I've been awarded the Distinguished Service Cross so many times the Army sent me a telegram in 1978: SIR, PLEASE BE ADVISED WE HAVE RUN OUT OF SHEET METAL AND RIBBON FABRIC. THE JOINT CHIEFS OF STAFF HAVE COMMISSIONED A TEAM TO SCULPT YOUR LIKENESS ON MT. RUSHMORE. CONGRATULATIONS AND GOD BLESS THE UNITED STATES OF AMERICA.

The Silver Star is the 3rd highest medal awarded for gallantry in combat. I keep all twohundredfifty thousand, one for every citizen in Dentville Wisconsin, in six hundred solid oak treasure chests. On rainy days I'll open the lid of one such chest, scoop my hands deep into the glistening pile, lift hard with all my strength, hurl them high into the air. When the fog is thick the tinkling stars shower down, winking; it reminds me of the Milky Way.

Do not doubt me. You have my word this is all terribly true. As a matter of further documented fact, I was no ordinary medic during those dim days of yesteryear. No sir. No mam. I performed brain surgery in the dark, without out anesthetic, twelve men at a time. I reversed the blood flow of an entire platoon to obtain the elemen of surprise. I called in B 52 strikes with my sinus cavity to broadcast outgoing signals. I was born in a bomb crater on the 3rd of July. In my pack I carried entire battalions of tanks and cannons; slogging thru jungle, the rotor blades of helicopters poked out from beneath my helmet, snagged on clouds, slowed me down. I fired my M 16 eighty two trillion times. It never once jammed or malfunctioned. I dug eight hundred forty seven thousand foxholes, pissed six hundred million gallons of highly toxic piss, I ate two hundred billion tons of C rations: I defecated four hundred million metric tons of highly enriched Government Issued poo. A not unmodest sum, don't you think?

Anyone can say they were in Vietnam. But I'm the real McCoy, the genuine article, I have the medals and papers to prove it. Meet me in Secaucus, NJ tomorrow at 2:30 in the afternoon, I'll give you a tour. Those under eighteen will not be admitted.

Marc Levy

The Second Coming

1.

The second coming arrived on Broadway and 42nd Street just before New Years Eve. He stood in his robe, scraggly beard and sandals, appearing a little dazed, or maybe just ethereal. He looked like he belonged there.

"Where is this place?" he asked a passerby in Times Square. "What!" said the incredulous man. "Who the fuck are you?" "Jesus," said the second coming. "Hey," said the incredulous man, "no need to curse, but you do look like him." He directed the second coming to Madison Ave.

The second coming stepped out of a cab on Madison a few blocks from Grand Central Station. He had no money, but even a New York City cab driver respects a good miracle. A sign said, "The J. Walter Thompson Agency." The second coming entered.

Sitting before the man who would become his agent, the second coming explained about God and Salvation and Peace and how much God loved purple flowers. The agent thought he was nuts. But there was something compelling about this man in his robe, scraggly beard and sandals, appearing a little dazed, or maybe just ethereal.

"Maybe we should call the Pope," said the agent. "Who?" asked the second coming. "It's too complicated to explain. Maybe we should call a news conference."

The agent called The New York Times and The New York Post and The Washington Post and The Daily News and The National Enquirer, The American Spectator, ABC, NBC, CBS, CNN, The Christian Broadcasting Network, The Christian Science Monitor, various Web site providers, the White House, and his mother.

The second coming and his agent stepped out of a cab in front of St. Patrick's Cathedral (it was the agent's idea).
The second coming looked at the tall spired building.
The cross made him wince. He looked down at his feet, rubbed his hands together, scratched his forehead.

"Where is this place?" asked the second coming. "St. Patrick's Cathedral," said the agent. "It's a church." "A what?" "It's too complicated to explain."

It was a slow news day, so lots of reporters came for the second coming.
They brought notebooks and tape recorders and microphones on boom
stands and cameras, satellite uplinks technicians, toys and perfect haircuts.

The second coming stood on the steps of St. Patrick's Cathedral. He
explained about God and Salvation and Peace and how much
God loved purple flowers.

The reporters held their notebooks like they were covering a stump speech,
but there was something compelling about this man in his robe, scraggly
beard and sandals, appearing a little dazed, or maybe just ethereal.

"What's your position on abortion?" someone asked. "On what?" asked
the second coming. "Baby killing," said the man from The Christian
Broadcasting Network. "It's a sin to kill babies."

And the headline read: "The Second Coming Has Come,
Condemns Abortion." The agent was pleased with the coverage. The
second coming was confused.

An editorial in The New York Times cautioned.
The Christian Science Monitor applauded. USA Today
ran an eight-inch story with color charts of Jerusalem
and Bethlehem. CNN tried to get him on Larry King Live.
Someone called the President and the Vatican.

The agent booked a suite at the Trump Plaza.
The second coming preferred to sleep with the homeless
on a steam grate in front of Tiffany's. He talked
to the homeless of God and Salvation and Peace
and how much God loves purple flowers, until
a policeman rousted him and said he couldn't sleep there.
So he slept on a bench in Central Park.

   2.
The second coming was not good news to the Vatican. The Pope made
oblique, noncommittal statements about "this figure who has appeared"
and tried to keep his options open. He worried.

The President weighed the political benefits of embracing
the second coming, and the possibility that
the second coming was a scam. He knew about scams.

The President ordered the FBI to do a background check
on the second coming's agent and the CIA to look for coded messages
in his words about God and Salvation and Peace and how much
God loved purple flowers. He worried.

The Christian Coalition liked his stance on abortion, so embraced him
immediately. They printed millions of voter guides with a check box for
which candidates supported the second coming and which ones did not.
They didn't worry. They felt righteous.

The media fumed because the second coming didn't do interviews. So they
interviewed scholars and pundits, rabbis and priests, monks and nuns, and
mothers superior. Peter Jennings walked through virtual reality sets of
Jerusalem and Bethlehem. Geraldo called it "the greatest story since O.J."
Steven Bochco plotted the TV series. The networks looked for sponsors.

Birkenstock brought out a new line of sandals like the ones the second
coming wore. Ralph Loren marketed a now familiar looking robe.
Trendy students and rock n' rollers grew scraggly beards and hung out
at Tower Records. Kids went to school with second coming lunchboxes.
The agent collected royalties. The second coming slept in Central Park
and attracted crowds.

3.
The second coming made the agent nervous. The agent experienced
a spiritual awakening. He started to spend more time in Central Park
and less time at second coming headquarters in his Plaza suite. The agent
still wore his blue suit, white shirt, red tie and black shoes, but he thought
of giving up his cellular phone and his beeper.

The agent tried to get the second coming to read The New York Times
and watch CNN. The second coming listened to the homeless who came
to hear him talk about God and Salvation and Peace and how much
God loved purple flowers.

4.
The second coming's second news conference drew reporters from
around the world. They brought notebooks and tape recorders and
microphones on boom stands and cameras, satellite uplinks technicians,
toys and perfect haircuts. They snarled traffic all over Manhattan.

"Would you clarify your position on abortion?" a reporter asked.
"I have no position on abortion," said the second coming. "But it was

reported that you said..." "That was incorrect. My agent will supply you with a transcript." The second coming was no longer confused.

A Gnostic scholar asked, "Can you put an end to speculation that you had relations with Mary Magdalene?" "Yes, I can," said the second coming. The crowd leaned forward. "Stop speculating."

"The Pope has refused to declare that you are the legitimate second coming." "Render unto the Pope what is the Pope's. When he leaves his castle and gets down here in the streets with the rest of us, then he'll have an opinion worth considering."

Asked about welfare reform, he said: "We should not turn our backs on the poor." On the Middle East: "Those people have never gotten along." On Rwanda: "Feed the people and there will be peace." On Newt Gingrich and Bill Clinton: "Father forgive them. They know not..." On The Christian Coalition: "They're using my name without my permission." On premarital sex: "Is this something new?" On homosexuality: "Is this something new?" On the current state of the world: "It's pretty much as I left it, just more crowded." "Why have you come back?" "Because it's time." "Thank you for coming." The second coming walked back to the park. It started to rain. Nobody moved.

The New York Times headline read: "Second Coming Slams Pope, Supports Abortion Rights." The National Star headline read: "Jesus and Mary: The Inside Story," which was also the name of the NBC miniseries.

The second coming appeared on Oprah and Larry King, Today Show and Good Morning America. He skipped Jenny Jones. He gave interviews to C-SPAN, The Wall Street Journal, The New York Times, Wolf Blitzer and Dev Null. His Web site, www.secondcoming.com, got more than a million hits a week.

Planes landed at Kennedy Airport. Thousands of people flocked to Central Park. The networks worried about ratings. The mayor worried about crowd control. The President worried about his image. The Pope worried about his power. He called the President on a secure line. The Christian Coalition was pissed. They printed new voter guides.

5.

Just before Christmas the stores were empty. Toys stayed on the shelves. Expensive jewelry stayed in its case. Nobody bought gift certificates for McDonald's Happy Meals. The churches were cavernous.

Nobody rode elevators, sat at desks, made important phone calls, sent
faxes or e-mail, negotiated deals, underwrote offerings, invested in
the internet, speculated about the future of Apple Computer, shopped
at Safeway, cleaned the executive bathroom, reviewed the R&D budget,
tweaked the distribution system, downsized, upsized or rightsized.

The Conference Board reported Consumer Confidence was at
an all-time high. Consumer Spending was at an all-time low.
The economy neared collapse.

The second coming taught from his bench in Central Park in his robe,
scraggly beard and sandals appearing a little dazed, or maybe just ethereal.
He fed the masses.

6.
The President never mentioned the second coming by name. He didn't
appear to be concerned. Neither did prime ministers, monarchs, bishops
and The Christian Coalition, who held secret teleconferences on secured
lines.

7.
The second coming knew the day had come. He did nothing different. His
hands started to bleed. His feet hurt. He got headaches.
His side ached. He said nothing.

The second coming sat in silent contemplation before a crowd of
half-a-million. Everybody prayed and munched on manna.

The second coming barely noticed the glint in the tree. He turned to face
God. It was like slow motion— the bullet coming towards him. He spread
his arms, looked toward Home. "Insanity," he thought, "is doing the same
thing over and over and expecting different results." "God, my God,"
he said. "why does this keep happening to me?"

Ken Siegmann

ahh...sweet utopia...

picture an American flag
burning
as it should

it's freedom of...expression...right..?

or maybe "we've" gone too far?
and maybe I shouldn't be saying this but

picture an American flag
burning
as it should

or instead of the Statue of Liberty
a giant replica of a plunger with the words
("Welcome Immigrants!" care of the N.Y.P.D.)
carved into the handle...

Felicity Sandburg

Something Vaguely Familiar

"Yellow Peril supports Black Power,"
The sign in the photo said
As Asian men stood among the Black protestors
demanding freedom for Huey P. Newton.
It was one of the many pictures
That didn't make the 75th Anniversary Edition of TIME
Alongside Martin Luther King singing a song
Probably much like the ones we sang at the SOA protest.
We, too, pleaded that we would not be moved
As I and 2400 other mostly white protestors
   were herded onto buses
By black police officers
Were kept in order and told to lay down our crosses
By black police officers
And for the first time I wondered what the hell I was doing there,
And what the hell those men were doing there
Because I knew Columbus, Georgia had to have at least one
police officer that wasn't Black.
"We shall not be moved," we sang,
It echoed over and over in my ears
And suddenly I hated everyone around me;
Because I knew that if violence broke out
   and there had to be an enemy,
It would be those black policemen
And somewhere the color of their skin would be mixed into it,
And so would mine.
Every civil injustice, every racial slur,

83

every imprisoned Black Panther was inside me that day
As I marched for those other "colored" people
   who I loved so much but didn't know
Tears ran down my eyes for them, but in the corner of my mind,
I thought that if a fight broke out I would take
   the side of those black police officers
And I'd be in Peril with no one there to help me:
A hushed and shushed Black activist in 1998 (?)
Time. It was $10.00.
I wrote a check.

                                        Tarika Powell

===

Date

I thought a Date
was a chewy fruit
with a seed
not
a pile of computer
profiles of love-hungry
locals with a clatch of
perversions, inhibitions
and restrictive morals.

"Won't you come out with me tonight?"
Has turned into
"Did you buy those super-thin Japanese rubbers?"
We have become unimaginatively dependent
on Nonoxynol-9
that slippery stuff that
makes it okay
never to have had a
senior prom.

It's more than okay actually
when your eyes get
large and bright
and we head off
arm in arm
around the lake.

                                        Steven Hirsch

Letter to Sophie

Garden
Parkway
YMCA
Dallas, Texas

22
November
1963

Darling Sophie,

Could it be only two months since I let your fingers slip from my hand as that train departed Voronezh station? I fear that this trip was a great mistake.

The boat sailed from Sevastopol as scheduled. Just two days and we were through the Bosporus/Dardanelles and into the incredibly blue Aegean and the Mediterranean. On September 27 we passed Gibraltar and started the long haul across the Atlantic. The work was not demanding though the ship was quite dirty and not really very pleasant.

We docked at Houston in the state of Texas on October 9. Defecting was surprisingly easy. There was supposed to be work in Dallas so I walked/hitch-hiked here last month. But I have not been able to find any work.

The people here, though friendly, are coarse and brash. The stores overflow with televisions, record players, mink coats, but there are many very poor people here too....

The great American leader, Kennedy, was shot and killed today, driving in his open-topped car along the streets of this very city.

My money is gone; my strength, exhausted. How blithely I left you and Russia behind! I feel my lips brushing the tiny hairs on the back of your neck, your nipples swelling.... Sophie!

May you know great happiness and love! I only ask that in the spring when you visit Krymskaya Pond, that you remember how we knelt there, how I whispered in your ear there, when the air is filled with the scent of its cherry trees, that you remember what we felt there....

Yours always,

Nickolay

Lucius

85

The Henry David Thoreau Volunteer Army

We're looking for a few desperate men
And women, quietness, no problem,
Willing to work long hours
With only intrinsic rewards.

The law abiding can apply elsewhere.
Must be willing to risk jail, poverty,
Death, and the vilification of the state.

Enlist anywhere.
Apply everywhere.

Goto.

Charles Potts

Poem For Your Birthday
To Barbara

This year both our birthdays end in zero,
Symbol, perhaps, of the nothing we'll become
Except as the reflections of our children –
Your boys, my girls – in the next millennium
Now so near. Who thought we'd see it come?

Let us reflect awhile on us, my dear:
Born fortunate, two creatures petted and well-fed
With milk and vitamins, thus our good teeth and skin;
Curled hair and handmade clothes and patent slippers,
This side of the moat from the desperate unemployed.

Ah yes!– and hasn't that come round again!
We circle back to the fascinating question:
How did we get from there to where we are?
We've perched on the edge of revolution, war,
I in China, you in Pakistan.

We both knew children who have died by fire.
We're yoked in sympathy for all that's human,
Having loved those of every tone of skin,
Having lived the loss of extraordinary men.

86

And the poems we've read aloud to one another!
You wave your arm in a wide arc of rapture,
Moved by the Muse, and another glass of wine.
I cherish that characteristic gesture
As you must smile at some oddity of mine.

To truly relish trivia in flower,
Woman-talk of recipes and clothes,
One must be aware of that high discourse
On art and life we could deal with if we chose!

"The flow of soul" as Pope extravagantly called it,
Unstopped, though years of parting intervene,
Though illness, duties, children interrupt,
We know we'll go on talking till the end

Or after, when we still reach out in thought,
Or waking, sense the living person near.
The password at the boundary is Friend.

Carolyn Kizer

The Politician
... a little charliechaplin man

As a wet finger held
to the wind became
this generation's universal
peace sign, mirror of mirrors,
the mere anarchy of polls
became truth's Tennessee jar
taking dominion everywhere.
Potter to president,
blended in one flood
the mother's milk,
the children's blood,
Herod come round again
as the people fade out
in one vast sordid movie.

William Boggs

The Ballad of Jesse Helms

(Expletives Deleted and self-
 CENSORED)

Kum, you sheet-heads, KuKu Klucks,
Klandestine Khristers, you dumb fuuks
 -NDEMENTALIST LEGIONS
Of Decency whose burning crux
 Inflames our nether regions,

Acclaim the name of Jesse Helms
Whose moral vision underwhelms
 -SCORES
That crotches, even oaks' or elms',
 Submit to underdrawers.

Behold this virtuous and reborn soul
Who rose up from his country's cornhole
 -PONE
Crying, "Let us have one sworn goal:
 Life above the porn zone!"

Driving out all that's crude and naughty,
He'll make our world safe for castrrati
 -OFF
And long-forgotten lines of thought we
 Hoped we'd heard the last of.

This saintly man from Carolina
Will douche the wet and wild vagina
 -RIETY
Of lusts, then purge us pure as China
 From thought and/or impiety.

Soviet censorship's in a slump;
Who'll tell Red Kumrads what to hump
 THINK?
Now Helms' Blue Laws give us the jump:
 No one will dare show Pink.

Both Ayatollah and Inquisition
Taught us a missionary position
  STANCE:
Hold still for our kind coition
 Or we'll cut off your grants.

Schicklgruber and Djugashvili
Died; men speak forth frank and freely
  PUTRID.
Facts. Jesse, firmly but genteelly,
 Will keep all knowledge neutered.

Our last, best hope – though some suspect
He's grown too old to get erect
 -QUIPPED
For the Grand Campaign that he'll direct
 To keep the engorged world zipped.

Nosing out all that's vile and heinous
He stuck his head in his old anus
  TEXTS
And found this creed: "We must maintain us
 One and one half sex –

"We'll simply order all the arts
To satisfy the same old farts
  RULES
That razor out the juicy parts
 And burn books in our schools.

"We'll jam our message right up front:
Give us no bawdy cock and cunt
  BULL, IMMORAL
Tales depicting obscene, blunt
 Anal events or oral.

Though evangelists and Senators,
Congressmen who frequent whores
  RESIDENTS,
Commit such acts behind closed doors
 And talk filth fit for presidents,

Now artists claim such rights; they'd share
Powers of committees that we chair
  -ERISH.
They've asked our aid. That's only fair:
 Let them have AIDS and perish!"

With chapter, verse and catechism
He proved he's got the juice and jism
  PASSION
To lift us up from lust's abysm,
Whiteshirts joined in a new fascism
  -HION.

He'll save souls at a faster rate
With his crusade to masturbate
  -ER REALMS
Ennobled if emasculate,
Kept marketable and steered straight
By gunboats from our ship of state
 With Jesse at their Helms
  STEERING WHEELS.

                                    W. D. Snodgrass

========

End of Autumn
remembering Hiroshima and Nagasaki

It is the season of sunsets:
like a garden the collection
of skies blooms, then falls
one by one
toward the clarity of winter.

Sunsets gather like a harvest
of plums. Overripe,
they throw themselves
against time. They saturate
the sky with the scent of blood
freshly spilled, and sweet.

A lattice of stars will wait
in vain for vermilion,
for azure or orange

90

to crack its crystal trellis
or break black mourning.

The sun has gone.
It died this autumn
when the sky turned
upside down
with the weight of suns
and never will be right.

Bob Redmond

Enrich Your Vocabulary Now

> To use any other word than power is to change
> the meaning of everything we are talking about.
> —Saul Alinsky, Rules for Radicals

1.
What is bum
but a word the mouth casts out
spoken without the need

of teeth or tongue
bum: a hole in a man's face
only a bottle can reach.

What is homeless victim
but a double trochee
a musical phrase to separate
them that got from them that not
while keeping the expanding catastrophe at bay
homeless: an off rime to Jesus
victim: a sister to system

What is rat
but ribs & grease
antenna nose
little pink feet
whose offspring squeeze through the holes
humans leave when the city they've built
begins to decay

Rat: a fink or raton
all that's left
when a species starts
to eat its own.

2.
Polysyllabic.
A well kept secret.
Like the man said it can ruin your whole day.
To get there at all you've got to be looking
because you won't find
Arthur Kill Correctional Facility
on any map of New York City.
The only road out there first has to pass
the largest land fill dump in the world. Breathe deep.

Inside Arthur Kill the women who work up front
chew gum & worry about their weight.
Though prison encircles them
issues about race gender poverty
have not caused a violent reaction yet.
They're (nouns) civil servants:
understaffed overworked grade 5 salary
(what the inmates call chump change)
an hourly rate that begets a forgetfulness
keeping certain facts away like let's say after they
(verbs) punch out make dinner for the kids
phone their ex for the check never sent
they go back the next morning to (nouns in the plural) 800 men
whose lives of crime they file & re-file 8 hours a day 50 weeks
a year 20 years til tired dead or deadtired & retired.
Those (nouns in the singular) men do get lonely for love.

Once in awhile worlds will collide.
A convict on the porter crew
just a kid doing a skid bid
(down long enough to worry
about the softness of a woman's skin)
looks up from his mop and pail.
In the accident that two panicked glances make
(beyond the fear that harm hatred
shame & blame will be exchanged)

there by the copy machine
they pause that extra second to witness
(adjectives) the same slow tender undeniable
need to love & be loved
in a face buried beneath a busy bee-hived beauty parlored hair-do
in a face below an ordered corn row concealed by a red do-rag.

Arthur: no one knows who Arthur is was or will be;
Kill: (verb) or in Dutch: a stream
 though there is no stream only factory backwater
 ancient hulls rising when the tide ebbs;
Correctional: (euphemism) implying a moral order somewhere;
Facility: exactly what is taken away.
Meanwhile barges of garbage warm up in the sun
waiting to break open
an engineer's idea of what can be contained.
Strike out for love?
 Poison the air?
  Locate what we've been told
isn't there? Let's just say
dying to enrich our vocabulary.

Kirpal Gordon

Whale Ivory

If I buy a tooth, a jawbone of a whale
carved, engraved, colored by brushing ink
into the lines, scrimshawed
they will tissue paper, box and mail it

it wasn't the craftsman, they assure me
who deftly practiced how to strike
at a suckling baby, kill it slowly
keep it shrieking
so he could easily spear
the mother and bull who couldn't
—wouldn't leave

it wasn't the artisan that kept torturing
to make the babies cry out
keep the others nearby, milling helplessly
as they tried to protect the calves

William Blake said
we should go to heaven for form
and hell for energy
and marry the two

I say earbones of whales, hand painted
still in tissue paper, boxed
says it much better.

Eileen Malone

Blueprint

A dying birch reminds a kid on the bus
of better times; he takes note and yells as if insulted,
*just think how many skyscrapers had to be knocked down
to plant stupid old trees in Central Park.*

Offices subdivide the sky,
desktop kingdoms of the city,
summer/winter blown off as perpetual spring.
One building keeps its old brass elevator
to recall for generations the swoon of altitude:
The whole carcass swaying up in a breezy, golden basket,
up through a shaft,
dark plunge in the heart of a building.

Once arrows flew from the trees,
bloodlettings to stop the heart cold.
And years from there,
war's chilly bombardiers let loose.
Silver drops flowered the sky,
then the grounded, red explosions.
Blackouts. Shades down,
light put out
like the suddenly disowned spirit.

Katherine Soniat

Sarajevo

an old woman
drags branches cut
from the grave
yard over ice
for firewood
shelled buildings
are stripped of
anything that
burns: beams,
floors, roots,
wallpaper,
insulation
militia men with
chain saws cut
decades old trees
all night as
it drops below
freezing
the children and
grandmothers
move in for the
twigs. It's cold we
have to stay alive
Sarija Musiut, 19
shivers as he saws
thru one of the last
pines in the main
cemetery nodding
toward the frozen
mounds marking new
graves around him,
It's better than
ending up like
the ones here

Lyn Lifshin

The Houses of the Poor

The houses of the poor resemble each other
like the bellies of pregnant women,
whether shaped from palm leaves,
warped gray wood, twisted wire, cartons,
newsprint, tin scraps, caked mud,
thatch, rusty pans, cow dung;
whether placed in India, Sumatra,
Mexico, Cambodia, Jamaica,
The Nation's Capital, USA.
We stare, sneak a guilty snapshot—
preferably through a window
illuminated by a single orange—
convince ourselves such matters
need not concern us
anymore than the lives of the no longer living.

Barbara F. Lefcowitz

Chock Full O' Nuts

The Gap stands where
You took me for
cream cheese on date nut bread
my favorite sandwich warm in
then palace of heavenly coffee
where democratic counters gleamed
and seats spiraled to lift
my smaller self upward

Where, yes, in my lifetime
we were always seated and served
a black girl child and her mother
hanging out in empire city

Only you inhabit this memory
we, together in the shopping endeavor
nourishing and sheltering after that special work
for you, a pleasure I never fully understood

96

Where you offer choices
and soft conversation
I want what you drink:
hot black cuppa java
scant spoonful of sugar and cream, cream
poured from ribbed glass and steel containers
stirred by your stainless held just so

I eat the slender sandwich half, slowly,
mouth closed, chewing
breathing this in
we are out together

Where you pay for me
and smile

Better coffee a millionaire's
money can't buy.

Akua Lezli Hope

fuck you, i'm wonder woman

i have cinched my waist
to distort
and accentuate
these wide and mighty rolling hips
the childbearing hips you love.

i have worked my thighs into granite for you
because you like them wrapped tight and warm
around your neck,
my feet entangled in your

                                   long
                       red
                                       cape.

i have learned to accessorize wisely.
my stylish hipster ensemble is
stunningly draped in defense.
while my elegant forearm bracelets
provide a jaunty compliment
to my soft and milky skin,

they also repel your attacks.
fashion armor vogue for today's woman.

i have a magic lasso
because i have to fucking tie you up
to force your honesty.
i need a rope from another planet
to pry the truth
from your pursed and smirking lips.

i have knee-high, harder, faster, fuck-me red boots.
my boots have a voice
that essentially says,
"excuse me,
sir,
would you mind
politely
backing the fuck up.'
my boots are tasteful
and my boots are strong.

so when you come home from lois' at three a. m.
high on smack, as plunder has become boring,
conquer so sublime, sobriety so nineties... and you
quietly snake the keys to my jet from my utility belt
as i sleep naked and alone awaiting your form
on the mattress next to me, and you take my jet
without asking, the only one of its kind, and on the nod,
too fucked up to even fly your own tired ass,
and you crash my shit into an untouched tribe,
then talk a ganga shit 'bout saving them
from their primitive ways, never acknowledging that a heroin
mishap dropped you in their midst,
and then you begin to colonize them, control them,
in the name of progress, and then have the audacity
to tax them for that privilege...

i don't think i'm overreacting
"due to pms"
as you so often chide me
to be so bold as to say to you

fuck your speeding bullets
fuck your tall buildings
fuck your single bound

superman,
fuck you

i'm
wonder woman.

Sara Seinberg

Almost

Everyone I know just missed
being blown up at five to four on Monday.
Every one I know just turned
the corner and looked back
when it blew up, or took
a different route that day
and were a few blocks
off. Only a few
were supposed to be elsewhere
but missed the bus, or the light, or their luck,
and wound up all over Dizengoff.

Karen Alkalay-Gut

A Condensed History of the Reagan Years

Under rotor wash
he can't hear us
but he shakes hands
with kids in ads. That
puzzled palm
cupped to ear   flanked
by deaf agents   shipped
home by chopper
look. In the blank instant
before he's hustled
out of the frame   he grins,
shouts a crack. What a crooked question he thinks

he never heard.

It gets
so boring in Siberia
that Gorby buys
a blue bikini and
enters the post-
modern Miss Universe
contest but his philosophy
advisors suggest the cleavage
isn't real
but luckily Nancy
is in town to consult
the busty blinking stars
which predict Ron Jr.
will win hands down.
If not
she'll fax the Pentagon
and have our boys
napalm the ramp
perimeter. Once all
the bathing suits are toast
she'll win
Miss Congeniality.

*

The rat
gets loose and eats
the cheesecake as
cameras roll and Nancy's
dress in the Smithsonian
grows and grows. *No sweat*
the president thinks
his this year's model line says
so he jokes about starting
the bombing now
some humorless constituents
are not artistically amused
and the stand up performance
gets mixed reviews. A trap
set by rodent journalists
snaps. The press secretary
talks with a broken neck

until the president awakens—
briefed while slouched, yawning
under a portrait of Lincoln,
stomping off with an air
of grandfatherly grumpiness,
it seems he hates to have
facts and taste and sensibilities
fuck up his nap.

Terry Wright

Scarecrow
for Matthew Shepard, 1976-1998

To pull the trigger would have been too kind.
They broke your nose, crushed your brain stem,
battered your flesh till it grafted to bone;
left you burned, lashed to Laramie split-pine,
spread-eagled, barefoot, a bloodied gay totem.
The night froze black around a scarecrow alone.

A day later your body was discovered,
limp as the straw of a weathered bale.
You never came out of the coma; I pray
you slipped into it early in the night, hovered
at heaven's thin edge, unburdened and pale,
before hate spilled over to the light of day.

Scott Wiggerman

Chant for My Niece

I don't remember the kid
our family album shows me:
a toddler with funny little blonde pigtails,
wearing a pink pinafore in the sandbox.
I remember her in college, with a wheat-colored braid,
singing folk songs and saying
the chemicals that crimsoned maraschino cherries
were no good for me. When she was twenty-six,
Sue and a friend were hiking the Appalachian Trail
to raise money for the school where they taught...
By chance, they met a man named Randall Lee Smith. "Nice kids,"

101

Randall Smith said later. "They seemed
well brought up." The next day, Randall Smith
shot Sue's friend, Bobby, in the head,
then stabbed her to death...
Stabbed her twenty-six times...Now I stare
at her in memory, she stares at me in dreams—
sister to sister, both of us blind.
oh, say you can see
a speck or two on the folded map,
reddish brown flecks on the Adirondack chair,
drops on the corner of a crumpled napkin,
blots on the plastic dishes in the sink,
a blotch on the steps leading back to the trail,
a splotch on her sleeping bag, a spatter on the stoop,
splatters on the couch, a splash on a work glove,
a spray of spots on the portable toaster,
a skein on the back wall, next to the window.
Blood on the paws of a barking dog,
I'm beyond belief with bleeding and Blood,
I can't see beyond the surf and the surfeit,
beyond beyond I'm wearing her Blood
Blood like a badge, Blood like a burden,
Blood like a bargain, like nothing but
Blood like a tide, a flood, a decision,
the crimson choice of Cain and his crew,
Blood on the Bible, blood in the stool,
Blood like a telegram under the door,
Blood drying sticky on tissues and towels,
Blood on the tiles, on the bricks, on the ivy,
Blood like my sister making dinner alone,
Blood like a well, like a girl with long fingers,
a man in his twenties with a gun to his head,
Blood like a dark ship rocking at anchor,
Blood like a dog in a hurry for home,
Blood like a ticket, a phone call, a number.
a marriage, a mix-up, an opera, an outcry, a premise,
a preview, a silence, a soap box, a business, a custom...
down in the valley all of us stare—
bound in red rivers of bright yellow hair.

                                                    Lyn Coffin

Stones

In the beginning
the stones are put in the crib
by the grandmother, the mother,
the big sister. This is an old tradition.
The baby girl is encouraged to pick them up
everyday, in order to grow stronger.
After only a few weeks the stones are replaced by heavier ones
which she is again urged to lift.
At no time is the mother cruel
about the stones. She loves her daughter,
but she does insist that the baby lift them.
She does this by singing to her the history of stones
and how women along the Korean Peninsula
have always carried them.

When the daughter begins to wear clothes,
the stones, even heavier ones now, are loaded
into her small pockets. Walking is not easy
with so many stones to carry
but her mother is pleased
when her young daughter begins to adjust
to the weight of them. She loves her parents
and besides, by now she's grown accustomed
to the fatigue of being born a girl.

This is her fate, they tell her, to be tired.
She, of course, believes it,
because she can not remember a time
when she did not carry stones.

So, it's a happy time,
the moment her parents have been waiting for,
their daughter coming into womanhood, the full weight of it.
When you look into a Korean woman's eyes
you want to stare
at something far back, dark,
older even than the whole, sad Peninsula.

                                        Tom Crawford

Smiting Arbor Day from the Record

THEY HAVE DECLARED WAR!!!!

I urge you, ready your weed whackers, your chain saws
         and prepare for battle.
They murdered Bono and Kennedy.
They refuse to bow down before humanity any longer
as the gods of their destiny.

And somewhere, a cosmic scoreboard reads:

         TREES
         2

                  HUMANS
              20,000,000,000

                                        Haigan Smith

Hard Bargain

I am auctioning off my virginity to the highest bidder

and I am not being metaphorical here
I want cold hard cash for my tight hot ethics

I am sick of my virginity
Back in the day, when we were eight, shit,
everyone was saying themselves for marriage,
or at least college, or at least a stable relationship
but now I've got friends' little sisters giving
me advice on handjobs

I don't have to put up with this crap
I'm in college and if there is one thing I've
learned about virginity in college it is that
it is, at best, an anecdote
But not having an anecdote is one thing,
the reactions are whole other story

 All the girls with there,
'Don't worry, you're bound to find someone'

104

And the guys, and sometimes
these are guys I am interested in,
all the guys with there,
'Oh. Well, that explains a lot'

And I don't need to be putting up with this shit.

I am turning 20 in 144 days,
if there was one thing that I have learned about
virginity anecdotes, is that when you turn 20,
the stories go from charming and poignant
to depressing and pathetic
My plan, at first, was sell everything that I have of merit,
buy a round trip ticket to San Francisco, rent a car
and even though I don't drive, drive that car
down that dark, poorest, scariest street in San Fran,
the one that I read about in the Covenant House pamphlets
my mom would get from the Jehovah's Witnesses,
and I would find the youngest, most heroin-addicted,
wild-eyed, fresh-faced male prostitute, open up my car door,
flash 200 crisp one dollar bills and say,

'Get in'

And I wouldn't tell him I'm a virgin,
I would tell him I'm a nympo,
and I would take him to a fancy hotel,
and clean him up, and lie him down on silk sheets,
and fuck him like I've never fucked before,
because I haven't
ever fucked
before

But then, just as this fantasy gets good, I remember: syphilis,
gonorrhea, hepatitis A, B, C, the clap,
body lice, genital warts, crabs
And then it hits me. . .

Sell... myself?

Fucking brilliant

Fuck, I would be this thing, this whole
underground sex world thing.

Business men from Tokyo would be calling up business men
in Hong Kong, who would be calling up business men
on Wall Street, who would be calling up Heidi Fleiss in prison,
asking how do I get a piece of that?
Rich kids from LA would be logging in to www.hymen.com
for hourly updates. Entire Italian villages would pool their money
so that I could lose it with the town schlong: Ernesto,
with the enormous cock that smells suspiciously
like flan and is crooked to the left

I could get corporate sponsors:
'This defloweration was brought to you by Dove Soap 99.9% pure'
I could sell the rights to HBO
I would have to shave my pubic hair into the Nike swoosh logo.
And after it was all over.
And the hype dies
down, I'll sit in my 36th floor apartment,
and then, I'll make myself some tea,
and pull down the curtains,
and turn off the lights, and close my eyes,
and lie in the dark of room, and

try to remember
what it was like to be

a virgin

But, until then,
let the bidding
begin

Cristin O'Keefe Aptowicz

Crucible: Allentown and Bethlehem, PA

Billy Joel never knew us
beyond the convenience of rhyme.
We sleep in the shadow of dinosaurs,
tenaciously breathing. Smoke still bellows
from the Dickensian relic of Bethlehem
Steel. And men take their lunches as they
always do, leaving room for hope
between apples and ham on rye.

There are less of them now, these workers,
but there is life yet in the spans, the bones
of the valley. The wives hold novenas–
raise an incense of stew, a cold milk
communion, a slice of pie on the side.

They are selling this hope, these bosses,
mortgaging The Steel and its thousands of
pensions on bellows of air. We have colleges
now, diplomas that mean something
to the young when they leave. And they
leave– these clean-shaven fishers of men,
these local boys made good.

And there is light and poetry left to us.
Survivors, the good truth of anger slowly
rouses the giant who is hungry again.
Our six stomachs fill towards a bagpipe
of motion. We are more than the parts of
a well-oiled machine. We can fill our
demands without the burden of steel,
And come what may, every man shall burn,
burn himself clean.

T. Dunn

For Father Cardenal

She's a foot tapping
pen clicking
hair flipping
eyebrow raising
head rocking
teeth sucking
"Who the fuck are you?"
kind of 90's
kind of girl

and she can't help but giggle
at the man who reads poetry
in front of the room
because... poetry is stupid.
He is unfazed

so intent on his words
and the history they convey.
In broken English and in fierce Spanish
he wants them to understand
the conviction of liberation
and how in a true revolution
9 year olds may lead armies,
die for a righteous cause.
Mockingly she turns toward her neighbor
rolls her eyes and fakes a yawn.
From both sides she is shushed.
"Why should I listen to him?"

Rocking in her chair
she mouths the words to a song
hands never still, tapping the backbeat.
Like a point of light in the dark
my own eyes track her
and I blink at the flame.
She just can't sit quietly
and finally the teacher
with Mrs. Potato Head lips
leans back and glares in her direction.
Like the poet himself
she is unfazed.

He recites a poem about the beating of wings
against the bars of cages
and how when he finally returned
to the mountains of his native Nicaragua
so many young people were dead or disappeared.
During this revolution
it was a crime to be young
he tells the audience of high school students.
When he came home he kissed the ground
knowing it was sacred,
a "great tomb of martyrs".
"How can anyone just sit here and listen to this guy?
What is he talking about?"
Except for his black beret
he looks like Santa Claus.
"Where's my present?"

In a choking voice
the last poem is about a poet...his nephew
who shouts, "Free homeland or death"
and accomplishes both by the age of 20.
The word "death" has caught her roving attention.
"There ain't nothin' I would give my life for!
Get this guy out of here!"

He's a worn down
sandal wearing
gotta say it
Can you hear me?
inside out
out of time
kind of 90's
kind of poet.

"You can't teach me nothing!
Go ahead...I dare you!"

Elizabeth Thomas

Now

the new people buying houses
on my parents' street
are cops whose wives drive 4x4's
big as garbage trucks

mom likes the kids they're pumping out
like '65 but without cloth diapers,
Vietnam or Russian bomb

altogether ripe for something big
the fall, the apples
jelly beans, exploding pumpkins
grinning brookhouse troll

and a ton of steel still required
to fetch a quart of milk

Robert Bové

For the Upwardly Mobile Unknown Soldier

The last unknown soldier
who got found out
DNA, like rules
and regulations,
will getcha every
time

Perhaps we are now free to build monuments to unknown victims?

Joja

Children Of The Stones

He played in a turret-city filled with hate.
Chased shadowy flocks of stone-shitting pain.
Racks of eyes latched onto every move
and stretched his shadow
to the length of a soldier.

In seasons of time-shuttered doors,
he fought the cool imprint of despair
while his skin grew as pale as wax
wrapped around a wick of torture.

When he was 14, soldiers took his brother
and he felt his blood for the first,
unforgettable time.
That was the day he felt the tug
of the stone and its hot, sharp,
violent testimony.

The day the soldiers took his brother,
he learned the shape of his future -
which he threw straight back
at them. They dragged him
to a paddock by the lobes of his ears,

pulled his guilty arm behind his back
and jumped. Theirs was the kind
of cruelty only victims perpetrate.
He dreamed of sand and blood

110

and calligraphy while hovering female shapes
    tore strips off their shrouds.

His father polished three sweating silver beads.
His mother stitched stones into his palm.

Jayne Fenton Keane

Bosnian Elegy

Angels chanting prayers
against retaliation,
what will you say
in bombed-out schools
to the orphans?
Daily they ask
What is the lesson?
Above them the mountain
looms like an angry hump
on the back of the road.

Angels of thermals
and low-lying clouds,
guardian angels to children
who dream a paradise
for birds and kites,
what will you say to their fathers?
Full of bedraggled wings,
even the sky calls for a reprieve
from granades, erupting seeds
in a harvest of wounds.

Angels of time that breaks apart
in fragments of stars
like shrapnel in the dark,
tell the combatants
who widen the fire in a ring,
to remember heaven's clock
sweeps over the world
with merciful hands,
that all will be forgotten.

Colette Inez

America's Talking

How come
everyone's
a
victim
lately?
A dictum of disease
and dysfunctional servitude?
No one's at a loss
for the words to describe
the ills thrust upon them
by this rabid, ravenous
insensitive society, that,
collaborates and corroborates
w/corporations to smother
the artist in us all.

"Mommy beat me.
Daddy beat me.
My quadrapelegic, paralegal third grade
Catholic School dominatrix brushed against
my elbow–a
    n
    d the rush of ensuing memories
have crippled me to the point
of sucking off several government entitlements."

Help me Ricki Lake!
Save me Jenny Jones!
Oprah, grant me thy telegenic wisdom
to discern twixt Maury, Montel, Phil...
Geraldo!

Home of the brave
My fat hairy ass.

Mike Jurkovic

Ruanda, Kosova, Guatemala, Iraq, Bosnia....

Check the wiring
Unplug the shriek
Listen to the steel-wool voice
of the box poised in the kitchen
Leash you doubts
with little grins
yawns
nods of the head
Remove your glasses
Cough
Adjust the paper flower in your button hole
Become shut spring   smooth rock
as explosions
grow nearer and louder
Although bulletins are printed
in another language
broadcasts scrambled
news gets here just the same
and death grows a richer crop each year

                                        Ruth Daigon

Mysteries of Nancy

"Thus the very definition of 'sign' implies a process of unlimited semiosis" –
Umberto Eco, A Theory of Semiotics

Ok, so this Fritzi woman is her aunt.
But that's a cover, right,
since offspring means hanky-panky
and alarms and the cops
from the Comic Book Code.
So Nancy's like those other orphans
Huey, Dewey, and Louie, like Mortie and Ferdie,
even Jughaid has just an *Uncle* Snuffy Smith.
Their parents fill a spacious rehab somewhere,
smoking cigarettes, watching daytime TV,
and waiting for their beloved art therapist,
while swapping sad stories
with the Katzenjammer elders,

who no one thinks will ever get better
not even the social workers.

What marvelous coiffure my Nancy has!
That Afro sort of do (her sensible aunt knows well
she'll never get a job like *that*).
And soul-mate Sluggo, more parentless yet,
lives alone in lower-class digs
plaster cracks the icons of his holy poverty.
Like Goofy he's God's own simpleton;
he's always game.
          She noticed first his head and knew
the wisdom of that dear bald pate
with strange sparse stubble
(like Iggy in Marge's *Little Lulu*,
the kids call out they're shaved for lice but they no longer hear)
and Sluggo spurns Ig's castellated cap,
sporting instead a helmet, emblem of insouciant
recognition of the dangers of even this flat and vacant town.

One day she'll tell her aunt she's off to Sarah Lawrence,
move in with Sluggo on the far side of the tracks,

They'll form a band, and make the rent by paper routes,
live on kiwi fruit and coffee
in bliss beyond the limits of the comic strip—
they've burst already after all onto this page.

William Seaton

Borders

1.
Just before a storm
we sit on the porch.
You have been picking berries.
Soon we will go to dinner.

While the others are inside
I ask you how it felt
to grow up in Berlin
with the Wall dividing you

and in broken English
you try to explain
how you lived in East Berlin
and were on vacation
when it happened

you were among the lucky ones
who had a choice:
give up home, job,
possessions, friends,
go live with relatives

your father knew then
those in the West
might be allowed to visit,
those who stayed in the East
might never leave

so at ten years old
you started over.
At ten, at twelve, at fourteen
even walls were natural.

2.
We sit on the porch.
You speak in broken English
because, I say,
I want to understand.
Under my breath I am speaking
of Israel.

I barely know you.
Two days later
you'll ask my friend
if I'm Jewish, when I'd hoped
you wouldn't understand.

3.
The image of us sitting there:
Jew born three years
after the war,
German born eight years after.
We do not speak of prejudice.

I tell you, instead,
of my father
how he had a business
how the colored who worked there
who he thought his friends
unionized against him
how, when I was ten years old,
I too watched hate grow.

You explain it happened
bit by bit:
first they set up
separate currencies,
then a new police force;
though the Wall was unexpected
all the bricks were laid.

You say thank God
there was no fighting
—after the first months, that is

and I thank God
we did not live in the South
where there were riots
and my father would have been
among the first attacked

I am thinking of Israel,
how what Jews say of Arabs
sounded so familiar,
how what began as pride
got out of hand

and I wonder
whether to tell you this.
Uwe, what I should have said was
the borders are inside us.

Rochelle Ratner

The Men Talking

Benek doesn't hear your question.
He and Chaika exchange
a few words in Hebrew

the conversation continues awhile
on other topics, before you ask again
if there's been fighting here,
if their kibbutz was attacked,
it seems only natural
this close to Syria
and getting closer.

He laughs it off this time.
No, no, Americans have
a distorted sense of the danger
they get from the news reports

no, as a matter of fact
their tractor drivers wave
to the Arab farmers,
each man just working his land,
a lot in common

But he is thinking of Shaul
killed last week by snipers,
father of three children
who sleep in shelters
and romp in sunlight as often
as they'll see their father now
his own son in the hospital, wounded

mornings rebuilding a barn
burned the night before,
the museum they built stone by stone
from the old Arab fortress

he continues: yes,
they've been afraid at times,
fear's a part of life here
but nothing ever happens,
tell the family not to believe such things.

Rochelle Ratner

It's not a perfect world, but

Let us praise the Creator for delighting in gardens,
who grows Bahai gardens, Scientologist gardens,
Unitarian and Hindu gardens.
Bless the Creator for seeding gardens,
Zen gardens, Buddhist gardens,
Christian gardens, Jewish gardens,
Muslim gardens, all with boxwood mazes
promising a glorious center.

Bless the Creator who delights in wheat
and wild grasses, roses and purple loose-strife,
cacti and clover, and yarrow, who made
color-blind bees bring cross-pollination, color
to green flowers a zillion years ago.
Bless the Creator who rejoices in the living,
Who sorrows when His/Her creatures die,
Who rebuked the angels for rejoicing
when the Red Sea roared back into its channel
and the Egyptians and their horses drowned.

Hilary Tham

It's not a civilized world but

I want to bless this America who believes Nature
is a challenge to invent instant coffee,
instant tans with ultraviolet rays,
permanent press, deodorant sprays,
depilatory creams and hair growth Rogaine
internet sales and press-on nails.
I want to bless this America who believes we can
get anything anywhere with UPS, American Express.

Who believes in spare parts
for the body but not the toaster, says
"Cheaper to get a new one."

I want to bless this ocean of contradictions, this
America who wears leather sneakers,
leather jackets, leather pants, yet,
chastises others for wearing fur.

118

Bless this America who believes in liberty,
equality and justice for all who want it

enough to start a campaign, and demonstrate
in Washington's blazing heat, freezing rain.

Bless this America whose women insist
on equality with the men, and have forgotten
how to sew to prove it.
I want to bless the women who insist men admire
their brains while their sisters buy silicone
breasts and low cut dresses.

Bless this ocean of contradictions,
this America who believes in Free Speech
and the Gettysburg Address while pushing
political correctness and sensitivity training courses.
Yes, bless this America who rues violence and
loves martial arts movies, abhors killing
but insists on the right to bear arms.
Bless this America who tries to spread peace
and humane rights while exporting "Lethal Weapon"
movies One, Two, Three, and Four.

Hilary Tham

Father and Farther

Such waltzing was not easy. – Theodore Roethke

1.
In McNeil Island Prison for bad checks, my father worked to pay back his
debts. One morning, a few weeks before his scheduled release date, he
climbed the power tower for some routine line repair and touched a live
wire. Unconscious and burned, he fell five feet before his safety line
snapped taut.

2.
My father knows how to jitterbug.
How many Indians can say that?

3.

He attended Catholic school on purpose. There, the nuns taught him how
to play piano. He refuses to play now, and offers no explanations for his
refusal. There is a photograph of my father and his sister sitting side by side
at a piano. She is wearing a silk dress. He is wearing a coat and tie. Did she
know how to play the piano? I assume she could. She attended the same
Catholic school as my father. She died in 1980. My father stood beside her
coffin and did not sing.

4.

Late night, Yakama Indian Reservation, my father drunk, telling stories.
We had traveled there to play in an all-Indian basketball tournament. My
father was the coach. I was the shooting guard. We had a bad team and
were eliminated quickly. We camped in a cheap hotel. Four players to a
room, though my father and I were alone for some reason. "Listen," my
father said, "I was a para-trooper in the war." "Which war?" I asked. "All
of them" he said.

5.

My father drinks cough syrup
because he believes it heals everything.

My father drinks cough syrup
because he watched RFK's last news conference.

My father drinks cough syrup
because he has a tickle in the back of his throat.

My father drinks cough syrup
because he has survived twenty-three car wrecks.

My father drinks cough syrup
because he wants to stop the influenza virus at the door.

My father drinks cough syrup
because he once saw Lana Turner in a parade.

My father drinks cough syrup
because he is afraid of medicine.

6.

Of course, by now, you realize this is a poem about my father. It could also
be a series of exaggerations and outright lies. I might be talking about

another man who wears my father's mask. Behind that mask, he could be
anybody.

7.
Summer evening, 1976. Our father is thirsty. He knows his children are
thirsty. He rummages through our house in search of loose change. He
finds a handful of coins. He walks to the Spokane Tribal Jail which, for
some unknown reason, has the only soda pop machine on the reservation.
My father has enough change for six Pepsis. It is quiet. We can hear
mosquitoes slamming against the screen door. The jail is only a few
hundred feet from our house. If we listen closely, we can hear our father
dropping change into the machine. We can hear the sodas drop into the
dispenser. My father gathers the cans. He carries them back to us.

8.
Basketball is
a series of prayers.

Shoot the ball
and tell me

you believe
otherwise.

My father
shoots the ball.

As it spins away
my father prays.

9.
My father often climbed into a van with our crazy cousins and left us for
days to drink. When he came back, still drunk, he always popped "Deer
Hunter" into the VCR. He never made it past the wedding scene. I kept
watching it after he'd passed out. Halfway through the movie, John Savage
and Robert De Niro play a sick game of Russian Roulette while their
Vietcong captors make wagers on the probable survivor. De Niro asks for
more bullets. Two bullets, three. He knows the odds. He holds the gun to
his head. He has a plan.

10.
As he dribbles
past you, into the
paint, then stops, pivots

and gives the big man
a head fake, you must
remember that my
father can shoot with either
the right or left hand.

11.
During the World's Fair in 1974, my father and I rode over Spokane Falls
in a blue gondola. No. It was more like a chair. Our legs and feet floated
free. I looked down into the water. My father held his left arm around me.
He must have been afraid of gravity. Then my left shoe came loose because
the laces were not tight enough. My shoe would have slipped from my foot
if I hadn't pressed my other shoe against it. My father told me to hang on.
He was smiling as I struggled to keep my shoe. I had written my name
across the top of it. I looked down into the water. My father was laughing.
The chair was blue. It was 1974. The entire world was walking the streets
below us. My mother was dancing for tourists in the Native American
exhibit. My siblings were sleeping in the station wagon. Gravity. The water.
My shoe. I Looked at my father. He held me tightly. He told me to hold on.

Sherman Alexie

Objection Overruled
or you can always go to law school if things don't work out

He says the problem with teachers is, "What can a kid learn from someone
who decided his best option in life was to become a teacher?"
He reminds the other dinner guests what they say about teachers:
Those who can, do; those who can't, teach.

I decide to bite my tongue instead of his and resist the temptation
to remind the dinner guests what they say about lawyers.
Because we're eating, after all, and this is polite company.

"I mean, you're a teacher, Taylor," he says.
"Be honest. What do you make?"

And I wish he hadn't done that. Asked me to be honest.
Because I have a policy about honesty and ass kicking.
In other words, since he's asked for it, I have to let him have it.

You want to know what I make?

122

I make kids sit through 40 minutes of study hall in absolute silence.
No, you may not work in groups.. No, you may not ask a question.
Why won't I let you go to the bathroom? Because you're bored, that's why.

I make parents tremble in fear when I call home:
I hope I haven't called at a bad time,
I just wanted to talk to you about something Billy said today.
Billy said, "Leave the kid alone. I still cry sometimes."
And it was the noblest act of courage I have ever seen.

I make parents see their children for who they are and what they can be.

You want to know what I make?

I make kids wonder, I make them question.
I make them criticize. I make them apologize and mean it.
I make them write. I make them read, read, read.
I make them write *definitely beautiful* over and over and over again
until they will never misspell either one of those words again.
I make them show all their work in math.
And hide it on their final drafts in English.
I make them understand that if you've got this (brains)
then you follow this (heart) no matter where it leads you.
If someone says you're wrong, say this (the finger).

Let me break it down for you, so you know what I say is true:
I make a goddamn difference! What about you?

Taylor Mali

Switching Sides

I'm writing the poem that will change the world,
and it's Lilly Wilson at my office door.
Lilly Wilson, the recovering like addict,
the worst I've ever seen.
So bad the whole eighth grade
used to call her Like Lily Like Wilson.

Until I declared my class a like-free zone
and she could not speak for days.
And when she did, it was to say,

Mr. Mali, this is ... so hard.
Now I have to ... think before I ... say anything.

It's for your own good, Lily. Even if you don't, like ...
It.

I'm writing the poem that will change the world
while Lily writes a research paper about how gays
should not be allowed to adopt children.
I'm writing the poem that will change the world,
and it's Lily Wilson at my office door.
She's having trouble finding sources,
or rather ones that back her up:

> *They all argue in favor*
> *of what I thought I was against.*

And it took all four years of college,
three years of graduate school,
and every incidental teaching experience I have ever had
to let out only, So what are you going to do Lily?

> *I can't believe I'm saying this,*
> *but I think I'd like ... to switch sides.*

And I want to tell her to do more than just believe it,
but to enjoy it.
And that changing your mind is the best way
to make sure that you still have one.
Or even that minds are like parachutes:
that it doesn't matter how you pack them
so long as they open at the right time.
O God Lily, I want to say
You make me feel like a teacher
and who could ask to feel more than that?
I want to say all this, but only manage,
Lily, I am, like so impressed.

So I finally taught someone something,
namely, how to change their mind.
And I learned in the process that if I ever change the world
it will be one eighth grader at a time.

Taylor Mali

Psalm Zero

the democracies of guilt abounding
on the church frontals money view
Yea! though they bounce
we shall fear no rebound for a shiny ball
bearing will orbit our reflections and spin off
markets will catastrophically eclipse our earned
run averages FONTS! the size of which amazes
every third world over YEA! though I hail verily
the mighty tightie whiteys YEA! I say
to the thorney crowney brownies HAIL! I scream
out to the multitudes of the otherness messes themselves
abounding again against the church fronts then
get thee to a game cock going twice there three
strikes out equal is in pink or blue packets
bias is a yellow bellied sapsucker
'Twas brillig o'er the bleached by tide diplomats
detergents of choice rare roast beast common
as when lawyers and freedoms meet
EAT! the body denominator EAT! EAT!
rejoice in the juices and gravy we made
with dead flesh in the soup kitchen of all souls hallowed tureen!
GET OUT of my sight ye scoundrel
HOPE with your little mouthful of teeth
get thee to a curbside to await your will:
to love-o-truck flatten your tummy to an asphalt comic
strip TEASE from your hands some hole of virtue
to sew up all virgins in body bags
and serial boxing matches!
YEA though I stalk the lesser of two
evils I will lose my self in the fatigue
of my faithful sins. sinning. YEA!

Alice B. Talkless

Pinstripe Piranhas in the Loisaida

Double-decker red buses rumble on Avenue A
Prospectors are taking pictures of our ghetto
Freaks, squatters, homeless, artists
Students, poets, actors galore
Move out for the sake of quality of life

125

Can you believe it, writers around the fire sharing rhymes and wine
Agi and Jeff urban gardeners defending the Chico Mendez Memorial Wall
The mauling of East Village will start promptly at noon
All dives will close simultaneously
Orchidia, Sluggers Anne, Dan Lynch--Closed!
All the galleries - Closed!
Veselka, Odessa, Second Avenue Deli--Renovated!
East Village garden-oasis bulldozed by developers
The mini-mall will open in the morning, wall-to-wall mall
Equipped with two McPoison's, three Starfucks, three Tooth-Gaps
Bones & Kibbles, K-Fart and Geek-o's
Replacing the community with Eurotrash
5 Spots - Gone! Electric Circus - Gone! Fillmore East - Gone! Gone!
Gone!
Soon our village will be a franchise of New York Disneyworld
With fake portrait artists wearing berets and painting tourists
With fake rock bands employed to entertain guests
Scroll the graffiti: MALLING IS APPALLING
Speak-up, stand tall
Before the pinstripe piranhas devour us all

Valery Oisteanu

Sunday in Hoboken

Sunday morning
is floating
down Madison Street
like an organ recital.
A few blocks away
Puerto Rican families
load mattresses
and cut-rate furniture
onto borrowed trucks.
This has happened
every weekend for months
as block by block
is emptied, gutted
renovated and sold
as condominiums
to people who work
in Manhattan.
For myself

I have to meet a man
in Jersey City Heights at eleven
about another place to live.
But some things don't change.
A man tends pigeons
on the rooftop
of the building
down the street.
The smell of coffee
from the Maxwell House
plant on the river
is still everywhere.
Tommy Vezetti is still crazy.
Doesn't matter
that he's mayor now
and stopped walking
up and down
Washington Street
in mismatched shoes
with his bullhorn
haranguing everybody
on the evils of City Hall.
In the small back lots
strung from fire escapes
iron pulleys
and tall wooden poles
are bedding, brassieres
bathrobes and work shirts.
They flutter like flags
in the sun
bright pieces
of uninhabited life.

Christopher Munford

The Apple Was a Plant

Left deliberately
hung
waiting for our desire
that began fate on its
intimate journey, eating
away at us

Bonnie Law

127

widescreen version

to de-construct
     construction in progress
             A TAX ON SIN
or so thought   homeowner   onlookers
Syntax explosion in bible read
             with bullets
             and folk songs
             and ninety some odd
             lives of which
             said eleven some odd percent
             under age twelve and
             as many rifles necessary
             for a Texas ranch to qualify
             as compound
Prime-time famous sequels and so ons
  lets call this JONESTOWN part two
        JESUS SAVES
a flock of his own BAD-GUY HOLD YOUR FIRE for a fiery end
        Let's reify our ratings
              with Television lives   get
  what they deserve   WACKOS
             Waco
             Buy it
             Just Do it
             Pizza Pizza
             Super size it
             Refreshingly new flavor
             Cool new bottle
             Extra strength
             Ninety some odd lives
             Under one
extinguished
     for the televised version

                                      Edwin Long III

No Place Like Home

At a family reunion
my mother serves alphabet soup
The letters H I V swim before my eyes
I blink: my imagination
or a cruel cosmic joke?
Speaking of cruel jokes
my cousin has one:
One stockbroker says to the other
"I got IBM at 26 and a half"
The other stockbroker says,
"That's nothing. I got HIV at 24 and a half."
Ha Ha Ha
Buddy did not die
laughing

Leslea Newman

The Politics of Buddy

I.
Buddy and I cruise the make-up
at Macy's. I swipe a lipstick
tester across my mouth
Buddy does the same.
We try eyeshadow, mascara
two shades of blush
before a Macy's matron
whose face would crack
a chisel shoos us away.
"Is it a crime for a boy
to wear make-up?" Buddy shouts
"Or is it a crime for a boy
to look so good in it?"

II.
Buddy and Guy saunter down the street
a few beats in front of me.
They do not touch
but their heads bent in boytalk
is enough to slow a car.
Ugly faces leer

"Hey, faggots," "Hey sissy boy,""Hey, you goddamn queers."
Buddy yells back, "We're homos.
We're as healthy as the milk you drink,"
then slaps a fat, juicy
kiss on Guy's lips
that no one could possibly argue with.

III.
I take Buddy to Gay Pride
wheeling him carefully through the streets.
A woman bounces up to us
"Where's your red ribbon?" she asks,
fishing out her supply.
Buddy says no thanks
and when she insists he pricks
his thumb with her safety pin.
A thin trickle of blood
oozes down his skin.
"Here's my ribbon.
Is it red enough for you?"
Buddy holds his fist high as I wheel him away.

Leslea Newman

Drive By Shootings
a Judeo-Christian apology

I need some of my tradition intact.
Do people write cynicisms about Buddha,
Or Hanumann, just because he's a monkey?
Is it just that Christ is the most
Convenient scapegoat? Or that we've
Known Him oh, so well...Or that
It's easiest to hurt Those closest to us?
Exotic religions and cultures
Thrill me too, but last I checked
Vampires are the only other guys
Rising from the dead, beside the Big "J."
And it'll always be the Holy Ghost
To me; how cool, haunted by God.
Does he watch each and everything
We do? God, as in-dwelling,
All-around good-guy voyeur--

We're lucky it's just the heart
And its intentions He plans to
Quiz us on. That, and follow-through.
We better hope to God
He's good at follow-through,
As the 1900's wind down that
Mortal Long and Winding Road
Where even Beatles die by bullets,
and fame is as lethal an aphrodisiac
As it was during the reign
Of the Holy Roman empire.
Pull in the reins boys,
It's gonna rain tonight and
Without Noah's rainbow promise
Nothing will be swimming
For two doves and an olive branch
At the dawn of the 21st Century.

Susan Tegeler

The good old days at home sweet home

On Monday my mother washed.
It was the way of the world,
all those lines of sheets flapping
in the narrow yards of the neighborhood,
the pulleys stretching out second
and third floor windows.

Down in the dank steamy basement,
wash tubs vast and grey, the wringer
sliding between the washer
and each tub. At least every
year she or I caught
a hand in it.

Tuesday my mother ironed.
One iron was the mangle.
She sat at it feeding in towels,
sheets, pillow cases.
The hand ironing began
with my father's underwear.

She ironed his shorts.
She ironed his socks.
She ironed his undershirts.
Then came the shirts,
a half hour to each, the starch
boiling on the stove.

I forget bluing. I forget
the props that held up the line
clattering down. I forget
chasing the pigeons that shat
on her billowing housedresses.
I forget clothespins in the teeth.
Tuesday my mother ironed my
father's underwear. Wednesday
she mended, darned socks on
a wooden egg. Shined shoes.
Thursday she scrubbed floors.
Put down newspapers to keep

them clean. Friday she
vacuumed, dusted, polished,
scraped, waxed, pummeled.
How did you become a feminist
interviewers always ask
as if to say, when did this
rare virus attack your brain?

It could have been Saturday
when she washed the windows,
Thursday when she burned
the trash, bought groceries
hauling heavy bags home.

It could have been any day
she did again and again what
time and dust obliterated
at once until stroke broke
her open. I think it was Tuesday
when she ironed my father's shorts.

Marge Piercy

Too bad you came in late

Too bad you're so late to the party, kid.
The salmon was delicious. They used
to breach upstream in monstrous leaps
every spring, so thick you could
catch them with your hands like a bear.
You should have had the caviar
while it lasted. Sturgeon swam
in the Hudson you know. Cod
and lobster were so plentiful
we used to feed them to our dogs.

We had fun lying on the beach naked.
We used to tan ourselves oiling
and turning on the spit of the sun
till we were barbecued, then lick off
the salt. You'd get melanoma now.

Used to be woods to the horizon,
puma, foxes, trails you could walk all day
without a boot print before you.
Now it's real estate: tract housing, malls
superhighway interchanges from here to hell.

Too bad you're so late to the party, kids.
We had oil in the backyard fountaining,
we had coal you could scrape from the earth,
lumps of copper big as your head, rivers
so clear you could eat the catfish.

It was sure pretty country before we
stripmined it down to bedrock, shaved
every tall tree till the slopes were bristle,
silted the rivers to grey mud. We turned
the mountains into money and we spent it.

We are your fathers showing you the way
to live, to die. We program your desires
with images of slick and perk and porn.
We bequeath you nuclear dumps glowing
under the soil like sunken volcanoes,

water from the faucet that can melt
your liver, millions of guns and millions
of barbed hungers and spiked angers,
cities of rotten asphalt smoking.
Welcome to the future we ignored.

Marge Piercy

A Smart Bomb

Wouldn't want to be dropped. Might get
Together with other smart bombs to discuss
Alternative employment possibilities like

Demolishing old buildings. Then debate the virtues
Of restoration, at least taking them down
Carefully, to salvage reusable materials.

Several could open doors for all bombs: start
A mentoring project in the armory: old cannon balls
With the latest hollow point bullets
Listening to speeches about social conscience.

Soon bombs are producing art and arguments
Born of a frustration at the lack of opportunity
For smart bombs to make meaningful contributions.

Can you see young people expressing their solidarity
With bombs by exploding themselves in cities and on
Military bases? Or a bomb specialist joining *The View*.

Tommy Hilfiger marketing a line of
Expensive clip-on fuses for bomb wannabes who
Drink too much and go to bad movies

Before you know it, parents are giving warnings
To keep away from after hours munition clubs
Worried their children might get rounded up
By the government and dropped on Kosovo.

Brett Axel

Spirit Photography

Where do we reside –

in our beer commercials
or somewhere outside of them?

Culture's mirrors
are all one way,

but if the soul
were photographed
would it really be
so predictably vague
and out of focus?

Look, there is the ghost
of a hand,

a family of shadows
stepping out of the sea.

Romantics –

where there is only smoke
we all find someone we know.

Yet the clearly visible
is more mysterious by far.

Our own breasts, arms,
legs, mouths –

unrecognizable
bodies

we can no longer see.

                                        Elaine Equi

Some Things Never Change
January 1991

Today the Gulf War begins. Once again
I am reminded of notes I took at the zoo
in Buffalo, N.Y., during the Vietnam era.

They read,
 Outside the Aviary Building is a huge cage.
 In it, solitary and brooding, a very large,
 powerful bird moves restlessly along a steel
 perch, gripping with talons capable of
 tearing a human to shreds.

Attached to the cage is a placard,
 The Bald Eagle is a predatory bird which exists
 by robbing the nests of smaller birds, and by
 preying on weak or wounded animals.

Then adds,
 The Bald Eagle is the symbol of our nation.

Below that, a footnote,
 The Bald Eagle is an endangered species.

Maude Meehan

A Question of Time
for Rachel Carson who warned us

It has been said we do not pass time, time passes us.
We are aware that it grows late.

The winged creatures and the animals,
the roe of the sleek fish, all these are tainted.
Poison seeps into our children's bones
from the milk of cows grazing in lush fields
and the air, the soil, the water, are no longer safe.

It is understood that we are lied to.
That for long years these things were kept from us,
learned only by accident or mistake.

In clear tidal pools anemones draw soft fronds
into tight buds as the crab scuttles close.
But how does a woman swollen with child flee the
great metal insect spraying the air she breathes?

We are angered by avarice and deception.
The copper taste of insecticide is not so bitter
as anger that grows rancid when we do not act.

We are told there are levels of mercury,
of nitrite,   Of radiation,   That are acceptable,
that in war there acceptable casualty rates.
That to prevent war we must deprive the people
to add to the stockpiles of our genocide.

Maude Meehan

The Canonization of Bob Dylan

They met in Palo Alto
to study the meaning of peace
Heard through your songs
proclaim them the anthems
they are
Too readily forgotten
The anonymous street veteran's
face mapped with memories of
family and sultan lands
                and having a home.
Every mother's son walks
In measured Sundays.
This Jesus transient
walks to church and corner
stares at the steeple,
      at our hearts,
    and minds,
for hours and doesn't offer
comment on the similarity of
spectacles
weddings and funerals.
He hums "don't think twice…"
to himself, spare changes us
and we remember the

137

younger stamped one.
Play me in the keys
of media amidst the halls of
Stanford—
Sing the songs
For us today.

Elizabeth Terrazas

How to Be a Virgin Again

Drill hole in head.
Suck up brains with vacuum cleaner.
Open vacuum cleaner bag.
Pick through brains, find little dead men.
Squash dead men and throw them out!
Put brains back together as best you can.
Replace brains in head; sew up hole.

Judith Basya

Feathers Hurt

My daddy liked to tickle me,
but I was not allowed to laugh.

The old man next door made me spank him
and said I deserved it,
Then he spanked me — and called me
his good little girl.

My teacher liked ice on his dick, then he got fired;
My boss liked ice on his dick, then I got fired.

I like being whipped.
I like having whipped cream licked off my body.
I never allow anybody.

I like being handcuffed, but cops take too long to come.

Judith Basya

Handing Out Poetry

Handing out condoms
is like giving people
a license to have sex.

Handing out genitals
is like giving people
a license to wear condoms
and therefore have sex.

God
what were you thinking?

Handing out fingers
is like giving people
a license to pick up condoms
and open them and put them on
their genitals, assuming they
have a license for their genitals,
and therefore have sex.

Handing out eyes
is like giving people
a license to look and see
and register Cool shirt or
Nice hair or I'd like to have sex
with him or her or both,
and therefore have sex.

Handing out ears
is like giving people
a license to hear
and making them want to hear
beautiful things, like Marvin Gaye
in the background, and another
person saying, Uh,
and therefore have sex.

Handing out vocal cords
is like giving people
a license to speak, and say,
Nice weather we're having,

or So, do you wanna have sex?
And therefore have sex.

Handing out feet
is like giving people
a license to wear socks
which look like condoms
to remind them of sex
and make them want to have sex
and therefore have sex.

Handing out brains
is apparently not like
giving you a license to think.

Handing out knees
is like giving people
a license to pray,
to go down on those knees
and praise their maker
for every beautiful thing
they have been handed,
to reach past themselves and say
Oh god, which might remind them
of sex, and make them want to have sex
and therefore have sex.

Maybe you have sex. It's not so bad.
Maybe you don't. That's okay, too.
Maybe you will have a child someday.
Maybe that child will grow up hungering
for human touch like we all do, and will be
surrounded by disease like we all are. Maybe
that child will fold and crumble
under the only four letter word
that makes me shiver, the one that took
my cousin, turned him into a raspy scalloped
rip cage with lesions and a ventilator and no family
visiting, and could take anyone in this room.

Handing out condoms
is not the final answer.

But
Handing out lies
to children
is cowardly.

Handing out silence
is the worst form of murder.

Handing out knowledge
is handing out life.

Handing out life
is like giving people a license
to change and grow
and change and grow
and change.

Daniel Roop

The Bride's Terrarium, Overgrown
(Assemblage)

Fill classic fishbowl one-third full with long grain rice. From magazine, cut out pictures of bride, groom and (optional) flower girl and ring bearer. Sink figures in rice so nuptial pair peek out the top third of the container. Without obscuring the couple, stick white calla lilies, ferns and peacock feathers into the rice. A few blooms should soar through the bowl's mouth. Drape a blue lace garter around a flower and over the side of the bowl. If you're ambitious and handy, you can build a rectangular terrarium out of plexiglass (front and back 8' x 8', sides 8' x 6'). Hire a wedding party and rent traditional attire. Insert bride, groom, flower girl and ring bearer (suggested names: Marion, Rob, Penny and Sam). Sprinkle in enough rice to cover couple's knees. Plant babies' breath and observe while you listen to a compact disc recording of Mendelssohn's exit march.

Christy Sheffield Sanford

Now In Stock

LIVE!
One genuine, Authentic
Real BLACK MAN
(African American to our P.C. Subscribers)
Direct from a Major Urban Area
Available for Museums, Concerts,
Lectures, Readings, Films
(The PER-FECT! Companion for
Black History Month!!)

Used to being On Display,
Comfortable as The Voice of All Negroes
"POC Friend" to Hundreds of Liberal Wanna-bes
Eager to assuage their Guilt

Witty, Well-Spoken, Intelligent
(NON-BELLIGERENT!)
Safe at Parties, Dinners, Receptions
Where showing your Progressive Sensibility is Important

As an Added Bonus
He's also GAY!?!
–The Year's Hottest Topic–
And can bring a LOVER for Larger Events
(They deploy on either side of the room for Complete Coverage)
or can escort a Real-Life LESBIAN
for those wanting to live on The Cutting Edge
      DELIGHT YOUR FRIENDS –
        As he discusses Drugs & Crime, Sports, Music
        From that special "Black Perspective"
        BE THE ENVY OF YOUR ENEMIES–
        As they wish they had one of their own to display!

(NEW – Now available in a Conservative Model!!!)

All this for one Special Low, LOW Price –
Ask about our Sliding Scale
And King Birthday Specials
      For Order Information dial
      1-800-NIG-GAAZ
      (Ask for Reggie)

                           Reginald Harris

Please flush the toilet

"For nothing was there a why and a wherefore."
— Phillip Of Human Bondage

It is tempting, the lure of a
freedom absolute even if seeping
with the potential sores of
utter chaos. I mean Hardy
inferred the power that
spawned a universe inherited
tragedy so profound it— I presume
he meant the universe— could only
be a dumb vegetable. And
although I am unsure how
vegetables could be dumb— all
things speak to me in sensible
tongues— my gyrating eyes— like
those 3d glasses given to the audience
for Jaws 3— can see past the flat illusion of
whole. I am after all an Irishman, even a
northern one at that— all, or most, religions seem
to invent frightening stories for the end, or tip, of
the world,
the North— And I can see— even like Joyce living in
Paris with a map of Dublin in his head— those empty
boys— one now my father— peeping through
sights on a machine gun and wanting to
be anywhere but in a place like
Americans in Korea— guarding
and protecting the fucked-up stale conquests
of Cromwell and
forging their own meaning for steel fences,
walk-about mazes, and
bombs. I, maybe we, are a tad weary of
grand stories to keep us at bay. In one way or
another it all trickles back to a god built so
thick as to plug all the walls of shit from
emptying.

Marcus Slease

And the Children Cried

In the fiery onslaught
of a technocratic firepower
Amid the high explosives
and computerized
guidance systems
In hell's crescendo and
the devil's design
A country
joined the ranks of
despots
A desperate leader
issued the order
to redeem
himself
To try and change
direction
The devil's design to
alter history
for personal gain
Two thousand pounds
of high explosives
on a child's head
Burned and tortured
innocence
Victim of a
man's delusions
Grandeur his aim and
manipulation his
folly
And the pitiful whimpers
of children
burning in his hell
The protests of
the people, the parents
The peace lovers and
the caring
Unheard, unheeded
In the frenzy of firepower
Evil against evil
And the children cried
in anguish and pain

Michael David Coffey

Back Home

A friend tells me of soup kitchens
and his work with the dying, those
whose eyes are bulbous with fear
of the here and beyond. "It's not all
in India," he says, and I agree (though
thinking of Calcutta), and I give
him ten bucks to help maintain
a hospice where all are kept well off
the floor, in crank beds angled
like ski runs —with lots to read, ice
cream on demand, flowers in light
an abundance —all higher than the stone
and dirt floors Calcutta nuns stoop to.
But there's never a hug in this hospice
run out of two zoned neighborhoods!
For that it would take Mother Teresa
or some other saint, lifting a burden
in such a way that Love could be said
to triumph, while Death is not denied
the ecstasy that it longs for.

David Ray

Discoveries
for Judy

I've thought a lot about bombs,
the fission one, the fusion one.

Both such reactions take place
in nature. The sun was bombing

itself long before Einstein
and colleagues came along,

long before Teller made
a virtue of fallout, the deadly

dandruff of the universe.
The question I keep asking

145

is this: Has man ever
invented anything at all?

The cave man who contrived
a wheel must have thought

himself clever, but had a log
never rolled down a hill?

Heaven and hell were here
all along, I suspect, waiting

for humans to notice, claim
to have invented them.

And you and I, my dear,
are both heaven and hell,

though we make no claims
to have invented ourselves.

Under the sea lobsters
have been known to hammer

but not on their own heads.

David Ray

---

an open letter to Dinesh D'Souza

*Mr. D'Souza is a recent immigrant from India and a Harvard 'scholar' who has
gained popularity through his assessment of racism as a figment of the
imaginations of lazy, incompetent, and generally inferior Blacks and Latinos.
Mr. D'Souza's eugenics-oriented theories are the basis for his frighteningly
popular* New York Times *bestseller,* The End of Racism.

Accent dutifully masked
statistics dribble down
your weak brown
chin
misty watercolor racist bon-bons
pop from your parrot beak
pollu wanna be a cracker?
Put the kettle on?

146

Turn up the flame
beneath the brethren you refuse to claim
will you serve the tea
flavored with the spicy essences
of colored folks like me
will you dab the spots from uncle sam's
stripe and star tie
shuck and grin as you serve
mo' strife and scar pie
recipe tried and true as the
500 year-old myth of white superiority
you are quick to count yourself among exceptional minorities
how suited to this task you are!
how eagerly you've learned to toss others to the fire
just as long as you're not burned...
Or don't you hear them sneering *Punjab*
when your non-white back is turned

Sarah Jones

On The Death of Hitler's Secretary

DUSSELDORF, Germany, July 16–Fifty-two years after Hitler's death, a personal secretary to the Nazi dictator who remained with him until his last days in a Berlin bunker has died in a hospital here.

Gerda Christian, who lived to 83, rarely spoke about her work with Hitler. "What am I supposed to say about that?" she once asked. "Whatever I say would certainly be misinterpreted."

However, a German newspaper said she told close friends she had no complaints about her time with the Nazi leader. Moreover, while working for Hitler she met and married his Luftwaffe liaison officer, Gen. Eckhard Christian.

Wanted as a witness at the Nuremberg war crimes tribunal, Mrs. Christian went into hiding after being released from an internment camp near Frankfurt. She reportedly never testified.

Was Der Fuhrer
    flatulent?
Did a typing error rate
    a pinched chin?
Did Frau Christian suspect Der Fuhrer suspected
    a Jewish grandparent?

His breath – was it
    sickening?

Giving dictation, would he pick
        his nose?

Did Frau wish to show Der Fuhrer a little
thigh? Did you ask God to have him order your
lips with yours? Were you, after all, in love? (Answer!)

Come, Frau, was Der Fuhrer's farewell gift no more
        than a generous hug?

Pray Frau?

Saul Bennett

Picture Lilacs
  For Barbara, who said she couldn't visualize two women together

Armfuls of lilacs, wet
with rain. Nuzzle your whole face
into the bouquet. Feel the cool drops
on your lips. Inhale.

Picture the ocean
from a cliff.
Stand at the edge, see
how the foam tumbles in
and disperses,
watch this heavy water
undulate until you're dizzy.
Lie down.

With one fingertip
touch the flat petal
of a California poppy. Lightly
travel the entire surface.
Close your eyes.

Imagine sun on your eyelids.
Recall the smell of wild mint,
the taste of blueberries,
the grace of coming upon a doe
by a river at dusk.

She lifts her gaze to you
before she goes on drinking.

Imagine damp seeds sending out blind roots
     into the generous soil.
See the root hairs absorbing the mineral-rich drink.
Feel the turgid green push up
     with a force that splits rock.
Hear the laughter.

Barbara, open your eyes.
Look at these women. You can visualize
any two
together.

                             Ellen Bass

═══

Don't Destroy The World

I've only nibbled
the grasses of my lover's meadow.
We are early May
and clematis has not yet blossomed.
Alyssum, buttercups,
I want to hold them to her chin
as we did childhood summers
shining their yellow reflection.

And the great flowering trees
splashed pink as dawn,
waxy bowls of purple swooning.
Rhododendron. Magnolia. I've waited my

lifetime for this. Plums are yet to come,
the fragile bloom misting their skin like breath.

Let there be days of grainy juices
sticky on my neck. Let me lick the pit
clean, memorize each crevice with my tongue.

Don't
destroy
the world

because my child's five, because
she cries when she scrapes her knee
skin shredded, blood beading through the dust
and I can't help seeing every granular photo
from Biafra to Bangladesh, the mother kneeling,
holding her child against the stunning pain,
screams like claws.

Don't. Don't destroy the world.

I've never seen a flying fish.
I'm told they are orange
and I want to see: is it like melon or
rust or the harvest moon?
I want to hear their wings spread:
are they translucent?
and their leap.

I've never drunk hot brandy after
scooping snow angels in the blue twilight,
never awakened in the desert, in April
when the yucca is in citron bloom,
or felt the breath of whales
hot and moist on my face.

There was a time I
thought I couldn't take it: the bite of life.
I gunned the engine, swerved the winding road.
But I never say I can't any more.

I want the future
to extend before me like the horizon.
I want the blue sierra I planted
squatting over the child in my womb.
I want the thick tangled hedge
rich with blossoms and bees buzzing like a party.
I want that smell to make someone's
child dizzy.

I can take it. I want to take it all.

Ellen Bass

I picked a
leaf up

it weighed
my vision

I knelt and
placed it

almost
where it was

Cid Corman

To embrace
a tree– how
silly can
one get – yet

to want to
dance with it
the way the
wind's doing,

Cid Corman

No Nuclear Night, Bhopal ?

Turpentine grass grows over this cold steel town
its black fingers lick the blue sky
and the birds ooze down drip by drip
painted out, painted dead.
One night the sky split, spat bright blood red
colour killed us
colour ate the night
cannibal colour
glowing dust grows over this turpentine town
small birds scream at night in dead droplets.

Anjana Basu

games

he's coughing
Christ, he says: no one
will hire me.
they ask about the gulf
war and that's it.
they're afraid I'll make
their insurance go up.
hell it's just a cold.
allergies or something.
I know guys who
got it bad, he said
you know you couldn't
smell a damn thing.
20 years in and now nobody
will talk to me
about what I can do.
I can do a lot. done a lot.
I can't figure it.
it's like a damn game
but I can't find out
the damn rules.

      I'm helping him
      with his resume.
      he's working as a
      security guard in
      a grocery store
      busting kids.
      he was first sergeant.
      supervised hundreds.
      now security guard is
      the best he can
      get.

hell I don't know.
any war does it to you
      he's saying
      any war slices into you
      takes something out of you.
      even that thing in Panama.
      people don't know
      how it really is.
      their yellow ribbons.

we stress:
supervisory skills
supply systems management
warehousing
conducting training
personnel evaluation
systems administration
program development.
he fidgets in his
security guard uniform.
the collar is too tight.
I caught the end of Nam
was in Saigon in
the last days, he says
now you can go over there
and find a job better
than you can here.
least that's what I hear.
this damn game is killing me.
I offer him coffee
and write:
proven capacity to
function effectively
in a leadership role
under pressure...
in the section under
strengths.
but I didn't get
Agent Orange in Nam
and I didn't get this shit either.
whatever it is.
I didn't get nothing.
it's just a cold.
I hand him
another Kleenex.
hell on that road
out of Kuwait City
we wasted them.
man it was amazing.
he looks at me
talking but
with eyes strangely
unfocused like I'm
a thousand yards away...

153

we wasted them
from miles off
across the night.
on the scopes you could see
little burning
figures running.
no sound. no smell.
man it was just like
Nintendo.

Michael McNeilley

Liberation Barbie

I'm visiting Barbie again today
but I get so upset seeing her like this
with all her bodies frozen forever
in clear cellophane coffins
like Eva Peron on display to the masses.

Barbie's dream houses are cardboard
and her surfboards, horses and Corvettes have a
shiny shiny hot pink shine.
God, she must be sick of pink.

When I was a kid, all she could do was
hang out at the beauty salon
eat at the ice cream parlor
or stand awkwardly on a fashion runway.
These days she's a rap singer, a doctor,
or a Naval petty officer.
But she smiles like a porno star
no matter what she's wearing.

Ken's molded hair and painted
bright white smile look painful.
At least he has a molded lump for a crotch,
Barbie only gets a weird dent between her legs.

Behind real glass, wearing real silk, are the real dolls
with really big price tags
($295 for a Collector's Edition of the Bob Mackie Barbie).
One young mother,

fending off an adrenalized munchkin says
That's stupid. You're just paying $290 for the dress y'know.
and I know she's never paid $295 for anything ever
no not ever.

Across from the pink wall are the Other Dolls,
not nearly as desirable, but they try.
90210 dolls, Shani dolls, Asian dolls, Happy To Be Me dolls
with small breasts, thick waists and short legs.
After closing time, Brenda Walsh and Barbie hang out and
trade clothes, discussing late night sexual encounters
with Dylan and Ken.

Barbie's hair just gets bigger.
No doubt, millions of little girls in Mattel focus groups say
My favorite part is her hair.
Yes, I like playing with her hair the best....
So the hair keeps getting bigger
and curlier and blonder.
Pretty soon, you'll just buy boxes of Barbie hair
with no Barbie at all.

Nicole Blackman

---

orange on counter

she came split down the center, carrying
pink overalls and a vinyl tote. she came
screaming the end of the world.

Woman on the Edge of Time.
Marge Piercy saw her too. she, square
in corner of room— edgy in points.

she came three times to see me.
I came once to buy grain. twice to
see heaven. three times unannounced.

i came zipped up the middle, dropping
green cloves and a paperback novel. i came
whispering the chords of an interlude.

The Unbearable Lightness of Being.
Milan Kundera taps it too. i, sex

with a nightlight– melting in spots.

i came three times to see him.
he came once unannounced. twice to
my front door. three times silent.

he came clamped to the end of the world.
she came screaming into it. i came wet
with a novel and a broken cigarette.

Heather Gawronski

What the Guard Smelled
(Fort Barry, 1998)

On the sharp coastal ridge
he saw waving dry grass and scrub,
paintbrush and the burst of purple
buds swelled with new rain.
He saw no threat greater than buttercups.

He could hear the thrum of surf's
hiss far below him, and while he fingered
machinery metal a scrub jay in flight
reminded him of his duty:
"Check. Check. Check. Check."

On the breeze he smelled sea salt
and horse sweat, the same spring pollens
that loosed the new bee swarms,
and the must of his own nakedness,
unenveloped by anyone's uniform.

At the back of his brain, his father's
song. There's a bug on the break
in the leaf on the twig on the branch
on the bump on the log in the hole
in the bottom of the sea. What

was it like, to be born?

David Shevin

Sanctuary
Tucson, 1987/Hawaii Island, 1997

No sign of entry
but a light left on
in her car to give
each night a message for
the woman following
meetings at her church: at last
she gets it.

    ("the ceded lands dedicated to
    remaining native and non-disturbed
    swapped for a disturbed
    and non-native forest")

Nothing taken,
no one harmed
but the woman sees
faces everywhere of
the disappeared.
On her phone tapping
sounds a man who
tapes her words: sometimes
a recipe or harangue.

    ("the appalling war on
    medicinal plants and rare
    birds at last
    declared legal")

No tradition
in our own
lives will
can access
nor the far sacred
grounds to sus-
tain those of us
left thus.

                                     Cynthia Hogue

We Held Flags

For some reason we held tiny flags—
though it wasn't our choice, those striped gewgaws waving in our hands,
someone else's platform (but engined by our energy.) There were chains of
red fire trucks, men perched on the backs of white convertibles, and
sno-cones that turned out tongues blue.

I'm sure we didn't mind waving them—a flutter of blue and stars. But, you
know, we didn't ask to wave those flags. My mother wore what she called
her sundress: white with yellow roses around the dipped neck, a striped
pastel bow around the brim of her hat. She planted those red white & blue
props in our hands, marking her own platform.

People dressed like past presidents sat on their platform rockers, rocking
slowly atop their floats. Their silver-blue hair glistening in the sun. They
threw Red Hots and bubblegum to the curb-side crowd. We dropped our
flags to scurry for what landed on the ground—darting toward striped
candies, easily dirtying what was white.

A hundred men marched by in a celebration of dress whites, and, with
hands on hearts, people stood up on their platforms while mother bent to
tell us "God likes boys in stars and stripes."A snare drum kept pace while
shiny trumpets blew notes so loud we covered our ears with our flags, and
watched with fascination as the soldiers' faces beat red.

And so we were primed. Our skin baked a soft red in the summer heat,
little bodies sticking to the white collared shirts forced on us by a flag—
toting mother on a self-made patriotic platform. But did she really want for
us, in later political unrest, to cross the blue oceans to face our own demise?
Or did we just look cute, dressed up and striped?

When I stood before her, grown into the large men's coats, striped and
decorated, pressed and ready, my face again was red but not from the sun.
I wore my uniform proudly, stiff and blue, stoic on her doorstep, doorway
framing me against the white sky of Nov-ember. She appeared on her
domestic welcome mat platform. And I presented her with the product of
her other son, a folded flag. Tears striped her wan white face as she held on
to the blue, white, and red. The platform taken like a rug from under her,
blue and remorse for flags.

Jen Oliver

White & Wong

Hi. I'm Mr. White.

>   That's White and I'm Wong

We're here to discuss the difference
between us, the difference between
White and Wong.

>   That's White. We're going to get lots
>   of attention for no reason.

That's Wong. We're going to make
some interesting points.

>   Pure White. We're going to ask
>   pointed questions, then ridicule
>   the answers.

Utterly Wong.
There is no answer and that's the answer.

>   Almost White but not quite. If you
>   lean on the edge, on your chin and
>   your elbows, you will see the answer
>   where it lies, which is within.

Wong, Wong, Wong. If you see the answer,
why ask pointed questions?

>   I'm losing track of the difference
>   between White and Wong.

Wong again. The difference is as plain as
day or night, or dusk and dawn.

>   All White. All White.
>   I've been Wong-headed.

On the contrary, I've been Wonged.

>   Let's put things to Whites.

I know I'm White and I think you're Wong.
But remember:
Two Wongs don't make a White.

>   Might makes White, or at least it
>   might, if you don't go Wong.

Some Wongs will never be Whites.

>   The White side of my brain says,
>   "White," but the Wong side tells me
>   "Wong."

Wong you are.
There is no absolute White or Wong.

>   If you're White,
>   can we both be Wong?

>   Thaddeus Rutkowski

159

Maria

I met Maria in Paris
she was from Venezuela
and she asked something about antisemitism
I explained about being a Jew in Europe
being a Jew in school in France
about Vichy
She stared at me as if I was speaking Chinese

Then she came to Jerusalem
and in front of the western wall
I told her the history of the Jews
from Abraham to the Greeks the Roman
The Arabs,
and she kept staring at me as if
I was an alien

She didn't discuss, she didn't try to understand
antisemitism
She just thought it was a crazy thing
coming from a country where such a word doesn't exist.

I just hoped there were more people like her
looking at you like a crazy man
when you try to explain the hatred.

                                              moshe benarroch

==

It bugs me sometimes that...

...I left rice in the sink and went away for a week to come back and see
black spots on one end of each grain and some were squiggling around but
kinda cute compared to the half-inch thick milky white mothers' that were
in my putrid two week-old trash or the three footers down in the project
high rises I read about in the paper during the trash collectors strike to get
ten cents more an hour while their union leader gets fatter off his executive
cut. Raid had to make more money in Baltimore that week cause my
apartment is right next to the basement trashcan area where roaches dine
before their permanent stay in my Roach Motels. The first time I moved in
with roaches I was worried about one crawling into my bed, or worse, into
my drooling asleep mouth. With my lens out it scared me to eat kidney
beans mushed in with veggies can look like half-squashed ones. Now, I

don't mind squishing the little ones under my fingers but, as my splat limit gets progressively bigger, I wonder how unhealthy this less and less sickening practice is. It's easy to get desensitized, I thought, after the Grenada, Panama, and the Iraq invasion when I went into war mode and placed Combats in every corner of my place, reading the headlines, "The Allies Plan to Corner the Iraqi Army, and Kill It," as I did so many of those brown-shelled nuclear resistant bugs. In the five-bedroom house it was different– it was more of a team thing, except one guy wanted to take advantage of the situation so he didn't take the trash out his days and baby rats found their way into it like the army ants around, possibly, my stray unwashed sink dessert bowl. But those crawling black-dotted lines didn't keep me up like the bigger pale-tailed vermin scurrying overhead at night...

...a little parasitism can turn me off a place.

John Potash

Black and Blue

Blue's in front of me.
His gun's aimed at me.
And thanks to the handcuffs
There's no escape.

He's wearing chiffon.
Spaghetti straps, tattooed biceps
Swaying his hips like a hooker
With one broken heel.

Rubber bands choke the scrotum
Blue
The needles through the nipples
Blue to white
To red.
Red, white, and blue.

Turn the bitch over.
Blonde wig hangs upside down.
Revlon red-smeared chest hair.
Shaved anus, pussy wet,
Raped with his own black baton.

Naughty blue. He wet his panties.
Naughty blue. Suck me off.

Naughty blue. Purple blisters.
And acid
And screaming.
And castration.
And mommy please don't.
And mommy please don't.
And mommy please don't.

Oops. A misfire.
And a no money-back guarantee.
He cleans off his night stick
Puts on his socks and boots.
And with a handshake and a hundred dollar tip,
Blue's back on the beat.
Patrolling your neighborhood.
Keeping it safe
From freaks like you.

Rotten Mather

Semi-Multicolored Caucasian

The Mao poster on the side of the ghost newsstand
is the shade of Santa's nose behind
the windows of Botanica Corazon de Jesus.
And I'm suddenly winged by a snowball,
but my extremities are too wooled to think it
racial; blame it on my silent adult presence
crossing the teen-zone of Maimonedes Park.

An idiotic happy music is in me sans Walkman
and as I proceed towards the gothic huts
of Convent Avenue, a work song of snow
resculpts my face. Mofungo smell hits hard
on Broadway's white door & the true Urban Indians,
the gypsy cabs, roar on oblivious to signals.

A flame rips out of Edgewater directly across
the river, burnt orange on black, like Mao Redux
– his sly grin deformed by snowspots
& out of synch with the current dance.

Joel Lewis

Interlude
(Israel, January 1991, between missile attacks)

1.
gravity
left on the threshold
behind us

lifted
my feet rise
above the cold tiles

with your free hand
you turn
the key

2.
our shadows
do not disturb
the pale birds

on the Chinese carpet
unfastened
your uniform falls away

candlelight
flowers glisten
on your bronze thighs

side by side
our masks rest
on the chair

3.
like rain
you lightly kiss
my damp hair

then the shower
washing me
from your body

a moon
slowly wanes
in my palm

4.
arching from sleep
I reach—
only your musk
on the sheet

the cat curled
in the space
where you dropped
your boots

the key
turned
again
clockwise

Reva Sharon

Late Nite

The horror special effects genius
presents the fruits of his labors
to "Late Night" television viewers.
He removes the dropcloth to introduce us
to "Raoul," he calls it, "the thing
behind the window in *Creepshow*, if
you happened to see it," he notes modestly.

The camera cuts in for a tight close-up.
"Oooo, Gawd!" cries David Letterman, as
"Guhhh," the audience responds to this
scaffold of bones over which latex strips
have been baked to simulate rotting flesh.
The genius fluffs up "Raoul's" scraggly wig;
demonstrates how the eyeballs move,
electronically controlled. The mouth can even
be made to smile in a gruesome way.
Another tight shot: the pointy teeth champing.

"Now I am told," says Letterman,
"that this is a *real* skeleton, hmm?"
"That's right," says the genius, adding:
"The crates they come in say 'India' on them."
The audience titters. Letterman, incredulous, asks:

"Gee, I mean, isn't that *illegal* or something...*buying* a skeleton?"
Then he makes his big wink at the camera, chuckling:
"Keep an eye on your loved ones, folks!"
"Maybe that's why the crates say 'India,'"
mumbles the genius, getting a big nervous laugh.
The camera pans up and down the torso.

"Well, gosh, where do you get these, er,
things?" says the host. "A place called
Carolina Medical Supply," the genius replies.
Letterman pauses a moment, then says: "Well,
I suppose it beats going to 'Bones R Us'..."
Another big laugh. The genius shrugs.
"They have an enormous catalogue—tarantulas,
snakes, rat lungs..." "*Rat lungs?*" Letterman
exclaims, but the genius is eager to share
the tricks of his trade. He shrugs again
as the audience audibly squirms. "Well," he says,
utterly dead-pan, "They *do* sell skeletons
made of plastic...I guess they make casts
of the real bones. But the plastic skeletons
are more expensive than the real thing, and
if we baked the latex on the plastic....
the whole business would *melt*...." "Er, I see,"
nods Letterman. The genius fingers "Raoul's" ribs
and works the mouth with the controls.

After the commercial they'll be right back
to show us how throats are slashed in Movieland
and how the effect of a bullet fired through the head
can be realistically simulated by exploding
a condom filled with red paint for blood

Bill Zavatsky

Ay Texaco

Hey Texaco
Whaddya know
Ya suck the crude from the ground
but not from the words your execs expound
Blacks toil
for black oil
in Angola
Where Henry Kissenger's the angel of death and cola
Your workers, ya callem Black jelly beans
Ya piss poison on the earth, and speak so obscene
Me tinks it's your hearts that are small black beans.

Shotsie Gorman

A Peer of Bridges

Today Berlin is a shadow.
people are hunched over their warmth
from the weight of color,
or lack of,
or grey of.
In a whisper all language sounds alike.
In a crawl all people look the same.
Sound is the vision to hear
as is sight the sound of hearing.
Smell is taste,
taste smells,
touch is sleep.
Nobody wants to see
that there are no more than one.
We pull away
We undo
We walk
from how our bodies fit together.

Elizabeth Castagna

Another L.A. Story

The neighborhood has changed.
The watchmaker has gone, taking his Rolex sign
his collection of gold watches
—gold is so seductive—
moving his shop to his apartment.
He told the newspapers that
friends of the last three men he killed—
he killed five in three years—
had begun calling the store & threatening him.
Besides, all the publicity
had unmasked his secrets:
two guns on his person,
five others stashed under the counters,
never more than an arm's length away.
Precision machines, the watches.
Precision machines, the weapons.
In his place, a slight woman, a chain-smoker,
sells 12-step knickknacks
one day at a time.

                                        Richard Beban

Why the Dove Is the Perfect Symbol of Peace for Our Time

Truth is, it's so skittish that it flees
whistling at the slightest footfall.
Ring your camp with doves
& they'll hear your enemies
at a thousand paces. Better
than a watchdog. There's a difference
between true peace & being warned in time
to repel aggression; but our leaders,
timorous birds,
haven't figured that out yet.

                                        Richard Beban

The Blood Stained

On her knees she is scrubbing,
slopping water from pail to sidewalk;
scrubbing 'til sweat drips from her face
to hide among the recesses of the concrete
her brush cannot reach.
She scrubs 'til her arms ache
though, to the uninformed eye,
the blood is gone.
But she knows where to look
and sees hints of red hiding.
She wants it gone before
her children return from school.
They will hear of the fourteen year old
who died of a gun shot wound
on the sidewalk in front of their house.
She thinks of her daughter
still trusting as she hides
in her fantasy world of dolls;
of her oldest, a son, just twelve,
she sobs for, prays for, struggles with,
pushing him toward a better life,
imploring him to stay away from the gangs
with her heart exposed to be left
as just another stain upon the sidewalk
as he becomes elusive as smoke.

Penny Ferguson

Sowers of Visions
for Benjamin Ernest Linder

Ours is a time to scatter seeds of vision,
bring these images, the hues, and cries of people
together into that one light.

—John J. Coveney

I ache for what the world could be
my friend said, a man who can see.
He speaks for us vision sowers
us farmers of dreams.
The world is hungry,

for corn & wheat, yes,
     but also for rainbows
     & such signs.
I have a dream
     another man once said
     & his dream feeds us still.
But most walk asleep
to the edge of the cliff
& step on the dark hem of death
but do not honor her.
The dreams of our sleep
are cramped, nightmares of fear
& in our breasts our hearts
shrivel hard like old prunes,
the honey in our blood, dusky vinegar.
     It is time we woke screaming
crying the name of our Mother,
     seeking one another's arms,
          throwing off our betrayal.
Hey there, brother -
          hey, sister -
awake!
     There is work to be done,
          to be done in joy,
& the time be come for visions
     for new dreams
          green as new corn,
& and the cold metal of our guns & bayonets
     yearns for cleansing
          in the earth of new fields.

                    Rafael Jesús González

VISITING THE MEDIEVAL TORTURE MUSEUM
--in 1996

We hang on the edge of our nightmare
repeating itself in bloody rivalry
greedy for death.
There are those who will say
nothing can be done,
joy and sorrow forever in contrast,
creates perception, and yet,

169

this is a poem about the thousands of land-mines
that still explode every day in abandoned
war zones all over the pockmarked earth, land-
mines explode fire, kill, maim
cripple. Legs of a boy, arms of a girl are
blown to bloody pulp. A Vietnamese farmer
in his rice paddy never knows
when his plow or foot might strike the metal
which will kill or cripple him. POW!
Flesh flies everywhere.
Fancy fireworks and big noise!
And so, this is a poem about
The Torture Museum of Unnatural History
where human genius is used to devise devices,
forged of metal, carved of wood. They sit
under fluorescent light revealing monstrous pain
existentially inflicted on frail flesh of self-loathing.
A man's eyes are poked out with a hot iron.
by a man who hates himself or is paid to.
Genitals burned with stun guns.
Electric shock applied to the quivering brain.
Spikes driven through hands with hammers.
Fingernails ripped from the delicate fingers
that play Mozart concerti.
This is a poem about how much hate
of breasts and genitals,
hate of wombs and anuses;
hate of child,
hate of brother,
as Cain slew Abel in cocky sibling rivalry,
still breathes in you and me. Tribal
hate lurks in the brain.
This is a poem about natural order
fierce and unyielding,
sending flood, hail, tornado, earthquake
upon men who could bond together to build
shelters for children.
This is a poem about the bountiful gifts
of the cornucopia shaped like the feared slimy vagina,
mouth which *is* toothless though flowering fruits
spill to earth from bushes that sometimes have thorns.
This is a poem that wants to scream and cry and shed
torrents of tears for tortured slaves,
murdered, abused children, raped women,

hated darker men who die without guitars or slippers
defending territory,
whose teeth grin at our guilt from their graves.
This is a poem against all the poems that do not care,
that are art for art's sake, only, that do not grieve or show
poems that care to find some new way to talk,
this poem says to fear cynicism more than death,
says that a poem should mean,
not just be.
This is a poem asking a way.
This is to say
that we're dead
before we die
if we give up idealistic hope and accept monstrosity.
This is a poem that can't
be powerful enough to mean
what it is until the bloodbath of history
runs purple and flowers into roses
in the vases of grave skulls—
that ends feebly,
asking a question,
believing that a kindergarten idea like co-
operation can replace competition
in the world marketplace.
This is a deliberately naive poem that says
land can be made
to blossom with fruit enough for all,
can be kept free of explosives, radiation, poisons.
Diseases can be cured,
greed harnessed. This is a poem that says
there is a way
to bury plutonium in sand and glass forever—
enough food to be grown under the sun where
no poem can top the wonder
of the greatest poem
of all: *photosynthesis*, first link
in the chain that fuses us to the web
of all life churning in silent space
wet and yearning,
tears made of the ocean's salt
that come like jewels glistening
from the feeling heart
to soothe the scars
of our manmade murders.

This is a poem that wants to say
there is a new way
to ask dangerous questions,
or celebrate what's wholesome and comely
from the rocking ocean, a poem that tries to yell: Look!
Mira! See the leer dripping down
the face of God,
the children bleeding in His teeth,
the priest molesting the boy,
the daughter raped by the father.
This is a poem that can't be strong enough
to say what it wants to say,
that needs you
the reader to finish it
with fierce love
beyond
rage.
This is a poem
asking
you
to
help find a way
to end
the horror show
in the Torture Museum of Unnatural History.
Because
we all
die
to live
and be some-
BODY,
this is a poem that wants...

Daniela Gioseffi

Acknowledgments and Notes

Sherman Alexie is in *Best American Poetry*, *Ploughshares*, and *Prairie Schooner*. His books include *The Business of Fancydancing* which was selected as a *New York Times Book Review* Notable Book of the Year. "Father and Farther" is from *The Summer of Black Widows*, used with permission from Hanging Loose Press. **Karen Alkalay-Gut** has been published in *Tel Aviv Review*. She teaches at Tel Aviv U. Her latest book is *Paranormal Poems* (Tel Aviv; Gvanim). **Cynthia Andrews** has been nominated for a Pushcart Prize. She has had poetry in *The Village Voice*, *Medicinal Purposes*, *Longshot*, *and Aloud: Voices from the Nuyorican Poets Café*. **Antler** has had poems in *New York Quarterly*, *Kenyon Review*, and *Chiron Review*. His books include *Last Words* (Ballantine) and *Factory* (City Lights). "Somewhere Along the Line" first appeared in *The Sun* and won a Pushcart Prize. "Armageddon vs. Blowjobgeddon" first appeared in *Exquisite Corpse*. **Roger Aplon** is the author of several books including *Stiletto* (Dryad Press), *By Dawn's Early Light at 120 Miles Per Hour* (Barracuda Press), and *It's Mother's Day* (Barracuda Press). His work has been anthologized in *Outlaw Bible of American Poetry* (Thunder Mouth), *Young American Poets* (Big Table Books) and elsewhere. "I Carry the Dead" first appeared in *Poet On*. **Cristin O'Keefe Aptowicz** was a member of the Manhattan team at the 1998 Slam Nationals. She is a two time, Barnes and Noble Monologue competition winner and the recipient of The Haney Prize for Poetry. **Brett Axel** is poetry liaison to The Orange County Arts Council and a Parkhurst Award winner. His book is *First on the Fire* (Fly By Night Press). He has had poetry in *Princeton Arts Review*, *Heaven Bone*, *Longshot*, and *Temple*. He edits *Outlet Poetry Journal* and is on the editorial board of *Hart*. **Miriam Axel-Lute** is an editor for *ShelterForce* magazine. **Ellen Bass** is widely published, with work in *Ms.*, *Atlantic*, *Ploughshares* and *Greensboro Review*. Her books include *Our Stunning Harvest* (New Society). An earlier version of "Picture Lilacs" appeared in *Common Lives*. An earlier version of "Don't Destroy the World" appeared in *Sojourner*. **Anjana Basu** lives in Calcutta, India and has had work in *Recursive Angel*. **Judith Basya** is the author of *Who Wears the Pants* (Obsessive Press) and *Writing for all the Wrong Men* (Linear Arts Press). **Richard Beban** has been in *Los Angeles Times*, *Athena*, *Blue Satellite*, *Fishdance*, and *Neon Quarterly*. His awards include The Soul-Making Literary Prize. "Another L.A. Story" first appeared in *Scream While You Burn*. **Moshe Benarroch** has books in Hebrew and English. His work has appeared in *Penihelion*, *Revue Europe*, and *Xero*. He is a contributing editor for *Ygdrasil*. **Saul Bennett** has had poetry in *Amelia*, *Pudding*, and *Peregrine*. His book is *New Fields and Other Stones/On a Child's Death* (Archer Books). **Nicole Blackman** hosts a reading series at New York's The Knitting Factory. She is the author of three books of poetry and performs with The Golden Palominos on their CD, Dead Inside. **Dean Blehert** has had poetry in *New York Quarterly*, *Potomac Review*, and *Kansas Quarterly*. His most recent book is *Please, Lord, Make Me A Famous Poet, Or At Least Less Fat* (Words & Pictures East Coast). **William Boggs** teaches at Slippery Rock University. Among his honors is an Academy of American Poets Prize. His books include *Swimming in Clear Water* (Dakota Territory Press). **Roger Bonair-Agard** has poetry in Phati'tude and *A Revolution of Black Poets*. His book is *And Chaos Congealed* (Fly By Night Press).

Robert Bové teaches at Pace University. His books include *Nine From Metronome* (Pisces Press) and *Nectar* (Norton Coker Press). "Now" first appeared in *One Trick Pony.* **Regie Cabico** teaches at The Writer's Voice and Musical Theater Works. He is a three time, Manhattan team member to the Slam Nationals including the 1997 first place winning team. He has appeared on MTV and toured with the band, The Smashing Pumpkins. His poetry is in *Outlet Poetry Journal* and he co-edited the anthology, *Poetry Nation.* **Michael Cadnum** has poetry in *America, Commonweal,* and *Literary Review.* His books include *Heat* (Viking,) *Taking It* (Viking) and *In A Dark Wood* (Orchard Books). **Steve Cannon** is the director of *A Gathering of the Tribes* and the author of the groundbreaking, 1968 novel, *Groove, Bang, and Jive Around* (Olympia) recently re-released by Genesis Press. His poetry has appeared in *American Rag, Sunbury 9, Pulp,* and *Aloud: Voices From The Nuyorican Poets Cafe.* **Carol Case** is an emerging, Alabama poet. **Elizabeth Castagna** is an artist, set, and costume designer. She has had a poem published in *Aloud: Voices from the Nuyorican Poets Café.* **Joel Chace** is an editor for *Antietam Review.* He has been nominated for two Pushcart Prizes and has poetry in *Seneca Review, Connecticut Poetry Review,* and *Poetry Motel.* His books include *The Harp Beyond the Wall* (Northwoods Press,) *Red Ghost* (Perephone Press,) *Court of Ass-Sizes* (Big Easy Press). **Maxine Chernoff** is widely published in anthologies and journals such as *North American Review, Sulfur, Chicago Review,* and *TriQuarterly.* Her books include *American Heaven* (Coffee House) and *Signs of Devotion* (S&S). **Arupa Chicrini**'s book is *The Ancestors Are Calling Down The Rainbow* (Carl Mautz). Her work is in *Poetry Motel, Tomorrow,* and *Back Alley Review.* **Marilyn Chin** is a Pushcart Prize winning poet who's work has appeared in *Ploughshares, Parnassus, Iowa Review, Kenyon Review,* and *Best American Poetry.* Her books include *The Phoenix Gone, The Terrace Empty* (Milkweed) and *Dwarf Bamboo* (Greenfield). **Michael David Coffey** earned The Butler Medal in 1983 for most notable contribution of a young scientist to Irish plant pathology. *Will Work For Peace* is his first publication as a poet. **Lyn Coffin** has had poetry in *International Poetry Review, Confrontation, Prairie Schooner, Kansas Quarterly,* and *Southern Review.* She has won Major Hopwood Awards in every catagory. Her book is *Crystals of the Unforseen* (Plainview Press). **Jim Cohn** is in *Heaven Bone, Exquisite Corpse, Hanging Loose,* and *Colorado North Review.* His books include *Prairie Falcon* (North Atlantic Books). **Cid Corman** is widely published and anthologized, the author of countless books of poetry including *Aegis* (Station Hill) and *At Their Word* (Black Sparrow). His awards include The Avery Hopwood Award. **Tom Crawford** teaches at Chonnam National University in South Korea and has four books. He has two National Endowment for the Arts Fellowships. **Ruth Daigon**'s poetry is in *Shenandoah, Kansas Quarterly, Alaska Quarterly,* and *Atlanta Review.* Her most recent book is *Between One Future and the Next* (Paper-Mache Press). Ruth's awards include The Ann Stanford Poetry Prize and The Eve of St. Agnes Award. She collaborated with W. H. Auden on a poetry project for Columbia Records and sang at Bob Dylan's funeral. **Diane di Prima** is in *Disclosure, Paterson Literary Review, First Intensity, Mother Jones,* and elsewhere. Her books include *Pieces of Song* (City Lights) and *Loba: Books 1 & 2* (Penguin). "On The Way Home" first appeared in *Heaven Bone.* **Frances Driscoll** is a Pushcart Prize winning poet whose work has appeared in *Mudlark* and *Ploughshares.* Her books are *Talk To Me* (Black River) and *The Rape*

Poems (Pleasure Boat Studio) from which comes "Incomplete Examination," her poem in this volume. **T Dunn** is the editor of *Zuzu Petals Quarterly*. Dunn's poetry has appeared in many anthologies and periodicals including *Black Bear Review, American Aesthetic,* and *Blue Moon Review*. **Elaine Equi** is in *Paris Review, Chelsea,* and *American Poetry Review*. Her books include *Decoy* (Coffee House) and *Surface Tension* (Coffee House). **Martin Espada** teaches at the University of Massachusetts at Amherst. His five books include *Imagine the Angels of Bread* (W.W. Norton) which won the American Book Award and *Rebellion is the Circle of a Lover's Hands* (Curbstone) which received the PEN/Revson Fellowship and the Patterson Poetry Prize. **Jim Eve** curates a reading series at the Howlin Center in Becon, New York. His poetry has appeared in *Hart*. **Penny Ferguson** is the founding editor of *Amethyst Review*. Her poetry is in *Antigonish Review, The Pottersfield Portfolio, Canadian Author,* and *Tulane Review*. Her book is *Runaway Suite: Two Voices* (Hidden Brook Press, 1997). **Charles Fishman**'s many books include *Mortal Companions, The Death Mazurka,* and *Firewalkers*. His work has appeared in hundreds of periodicals. His awards include The Ann Stanford Poetry Prize, The Firman Houghton Poetry Award and the Gertrude B Clayton Award. He received a New York Foundation for the Arts Fellowship in 1995. **Fletch** was on the 1998 Slam Nationals Ft Worth Team. His CD is *Hung Like a Sasquatch* (Rainmaker Records). His book is *Bruised Sex and Bad Poems*. **Heather Gawronski**'s poetry has been in *Outlet Poetry Journal, South Loop Review,* and the anthology, *The Wandering Uterus*. **Daniela Gioseffi** edited the anthology, *Women on War* (Simon and Schuster) which earned an American Book Award and *On Prejudice: A Global Perspective* (Anchor/Doubleday) which earned a World Peace Award. "Visiting the Torture Museum" first appeared on *Real Poetic, 1998*. Her nine books include *In Bed with the Exotic Enemy*. Her poetry is in *Paris Review, Nation, Antaeus,* and *Prairie Schooner*. She has been awarded two NYS Council for the Arts grants. **E Gironda Jr** is a lawyer as well as a poet who's work is in *Hart*. **Jesse Glass** is in *Confrontation, New England Review,* and *Literary Review*. His books include *Life and Death of Peter Stubbe* (Birch Book Press). **Kirpal Gordon**'s books include *Dear Empire State Building* (Heaven Bone) and *This Ain't No Ballgame* (Heaven Bone). **Rafael Jesús Gonzalez** has been widely published in Mexico, The USA, and Europe. His most recent book is *El Hacedor de Juegos / The Maker of Games* (Casa Editorial). "Sowers of Visions" was first published in *Second Coming*. **Guy LeCharles Gonzalez** was a member of the first place New York team at the 1998 Slam Nationals. He hosts a reading series at Bar 13. **Shotsie Gorman** is a Ginsberg Award winning poet and tattoo artist whose work has appeared in *The New York Times, Outlet Poetry Journal* and *Hart*. His book is *The Black Marks I've Made* (Proteus Press). **Susan Griffin** is an Emmy Award winning author whose poetry has been widely published and anthologized. She has been in *Mother Jones, American Poetry Review, City Lights Review,* and *Utne Reader*. Her most recent collection is *Bending Home Poems* (Copper Canyon). **Donald Hall** is in *New Yorker, Atlantic, New Republic, Gettysburg Review,* and *Iowa Review*. His most recent book is *Without* (Houghton Mifflin). "The Coalition" first appeared in *The Nation*. **Janet Hamill** has had poetry in *Gargoyle, Kansas Quarterly, City Lights Review,* and *Bomb*. Her books include *Lost Ceilings* (Telephone Books) and *Nostalgia of the Infinite* (Ocean View Books). **Reginald Harris** co-edits *Kuumba*. His work has appeared in *Harvard Gay and*

Lesbian Review, Obsidian II, Pearl, and *Outlet Poetry Journal.* **Steven Hirsch** is the editor of *Heaven Bone Magazine.* He has had poetry in *Pudding, Outlet Poetry Journal, Etcetera,* and *Hunger.* His book is *Ramapo 500 Affirmations and Other Poems* (Flower Thief Press). **Cynthia Hogue** is the author of three books including *The Never Wife* which won The Mammoth Press Poetry Contest. She teaches English at Bucknell University and directs the Stadler Center for Poetry. **Bob Holman** is the man behind Mouth Almighty Records, the author of *Collect Call of the Wild* (Henry Holt,) the co-editor of the American Book Award winning anthology, *Aloud: Voices From The Nuyorican Poets Café* (Henry Holt) and the producer of the PBS series, *The United States of Poetry.* His work is in *A Gathering of the Tribes, The Temple,* and *Exquisite Corpse.* He teaches at Bard College. **Akua Lesli Hope**'s first volume of poetry, *Embouchure,* won The Writer's Digest Book Award. Other awards include a NY State Foundation for the Arts Fellowship, and a National Endowment for the Arts Fellowship. Akua is the South NY coordinator of Amnesty International. **Colette Inez** has had poetry in *Prairie Schooner, Ploughshares, Iowa Review,* and *Ohio Review.* Her most recent book is *Clemency* (Carnegie Mellon University Press). **Larry Jaffe**'s books include *Jewish Soul Food, Winter Rose,* and *Hate's Not Natural.* He hosts a reading and slam series at the Moondog Café in Hollywood, CA. **Jimmy Jazz** writes for San Diego's *Uptown News Magazine.* His poetry has appeared in *Damaged Goods, Cupid,* and *Carbon 14.* His book is *The Sub* (Incommunicado Press). **Jojá** has had poetry published in *The Canadian Jewish News,* and *Ravage* She is the publisher of *Blue Moon Anthology.* **Sarah Jones** was a member of the writing team for Broadway's *Capeman* with Paul Simon and Derek Walcott. She is a 1997 Nuyorican Poets Café Grand Poetry Slam Champion and a 1998 Van Lier Literary Fellow. **Mike Jurkovic** has had poetry published in *Hart.* "America's Talking" is from his book, *The Baritone Emeritus.* **Mikel K** is *Creative Loafing*'s Best Spoken Word Artist of 1999. His work has appeared in *Blue Milk, GSU Review,* and *Atlanta.* His CDs include *Don't Say Hate* (E Records). **Jayne Fenton Keane** is in *Social Alternatives, Free Xpression, Southern Review,* and *Idiom.* Her awards include a Varuna Writers Centre Fellowship. **Keystone** is an emerging New York poet. **Carolyn Kizer** founded *Poetry Northwest Magazine.* She served as the first director of the literature program of The National Endowment for the Arts. Her fourth book, *Yin,* earned a Pulitzer Prize in 1985. She is now chancellor for the Academy of American Poets. Her work has appeared in *Antaeus, Paris Review,* and *Michigan Quarterly Review.* Her books include *Harping On Poems: 1985 - 1995* (Copper Canyon Press) and *Mermaids in the Basement* (Copper Canyon Press). "Poem For Your Birthday" first appeared in *Poetry.* **Ken La Rive** has been published in *L'Intrigue.* **Bonnie Law** has had poems in *Orange Review, Outlet Poetry Journal, Algonquin Quarterly,* and *Handmade Poems.* **Barbara F. Lefcowitz** has had poetry in *Other Voices* and *Minnesota Review.* She has received grants from the Rockefeller Foundation and the National Endowment for the Arts. Her books include *The Minarets of Vienna* (Chestnut Hills) and *Red Lies & White Lies* (East Coast Books). **Marc Levy** served as a medic in Viet Nam and Cambodia. His work has appeared in *Slant, Peregrine, and Vagabond Monthly.* **Joel Lewis** is a Ted Barrigan Award winning poet. "Semi-Multicolored Caucasian" is from his book, *House Rent Boogie.* **Jennifer Ley** is a 1998 Pushcart Prize nominee. She edits *Perihelion* and has had poetry in *Mobius* and *Recursive Angel*. **Lyn Lifshin** is the author of over 90 books including *Before it's Light* (Black Sparrow Press), *Cold Comfort* (Black Sparrow Press) and *Blue Tattoo* (Event Horizon). She was the subject of the award-winning documentary film, *Not Made of Glass*. Her many awards include a New York State Caps Grant, a Breadloaf Scholarship, and a Jack Kerouac Award. **Deena Linett** is the author of several books. Deena's poetry has been published in *Charlotte Poetry Review, Harvard Magazine, Missouri Review,* and elsewhere. Awards include a Sweeny Cox Prize and fellowships to The Virginia Center for the Creative Arts and The Hawthornden Castle International Retreat for Writers. **Edwin Long III** has been anthologized in *Live at Karla's*. **Caldor Lowe** is the editor of *Montserrat Review*. **Lucius** is the creator and proprietor of *A Poetry Lover's Guide to the World Wide Web* and the assistant editor of Writer's Block. **Taylor Mali** teaches at Browning School. Two consecutive Slam Nationals team champion, he is featured in the motion pictures, *Slam* and *Slam Nation*. His poetry has appeared in *Hart,* and *Poetry Nation* (Véhicule Press). "Switching Sides" first appeared in *Underwood Review*. **Eileen Malone**'s awards include the Phyllis Smart Young Prize, The Dorothy Daniels Award and The Virginia Bagliori Award. **Lisa Martinovic**'s books include *Poemedy* (New Paradigm Productions). Her work has appeared in *Omnivore* and *Exquisite Corpse* as well as 7 anthologies. She has been a member of the Ozark team at four consecutive National Poetry Slams. "The Difference Between Breasts and Tits" first appeared in *The Chunk Ganoma*. **Rotton Mather** was published early in life in the anthology, *Rainbow Collection: Stories and Poetry by Young People*. More recently, her work has been in *The Journal of Liberal Studies* and *Outlet Poetry Journal*. Her books are *Scum* and *Peepshow*, both from Zeropanik Press. **Marty McConnell** has poetry in the anthology, *The Wandering Uterus*. **Cynthia McCallion** co-hosts a reading series in Warwick, New York. **Stazja McFadyen**'s books are *Dream Songs* and *If You Can't Eat'em Join'em*. Her poetry is in *The Austin Chronicle, Poetry Magazine,* and the anthologies *Di-Verse-City Too* and *Flirting with Crawfish*. **Michael McNeilley**'s most recent book is *Situational Reality* (Dream Horse Press) and has poetry in such publications as *The New York Quarterly, The Mississippi Review, The Chicago Review,* and *Slipstream*. **Maude Meehan** leads poetry workshops at the University of Santa Cruz. Her most recent book is *Washing the Stones, Selected poems 1975 - 1995* (Papier-Mache Press). Her work is widely published and anthologized. **Robert Milby** has had poetry in *Hart, Outlet Poetry Journal,* and *North Street Journal*. He was a judge for the New York State Department of Education Student Arts Competition in 1997. **Honor Moore** has received fellowships from The National Endowment for the Arts and The New York State Council on the Arts. Her play, *Mourning Pictures* was produced on Broadway in 1974. Her poetry has appeared in *New Yorker, Seneca Review, Paris Review,* and *American Poetry Review*. Her most recent book is *The White Blackbird* (Penguin). **Michele Morgan** teaches at Sydney University. Michele's work appears on the CDs *Passion Pop* by Coda, Darrin Verhagen's *Succulent Blue Sway* and *Tongue Circus*. Periodical publications include *Lungfull!, Anchorite's Diner, Outlet Poetry Journal* and *Word of Mouth*. **Christopher Munford**'s book is *Sermons in Stone* (Birch Brook Press). "Sunday in Hoboken" first appeared in *Make Room for Dada*. **Leslea Newman** is a 1997 National Endowment for the Arts Fellow. Her twenty-seven books including *Heather Has Two Mommies*. Her poems in this volume appear in

Still Life With Buddy (Pride Publications) used with permission. **Valery Oisteanu**'s books include *Zen Dada* (Linear Art Press) *Perks in Purgatory* (Pass Press). **Jen Oliver** is an editor for *Painted Bride Quarterly.* Her poetry has appeared in *Café Review* and *Poets Guide Quarterly.* **Alix Olson** is an Outwrite Queer National Poetry Slam Champion, a member of the first place 1998 Slam Nationals New York Team and recipient of The Barbara Deming Memorial Grant. Her poetry is in *Lesbian Review of Books, Advocate,* and *A Gathering of the Tribes.* **Amy Ouzoonian** has been in *Outlet Poetry Journal, Hart, Word on the Street,* and *Orange Review.* She is an editor for *A Gathering of the Tribes.* Her chapbook is *Inkubaiting Estrogin.* "She Won't Say She's Unhappy" first appeared in *Skyscrapers, Taxis, and Tampons* (Fly By Night Press). **James Owens** is in *Sow's Ear, Poem,* and *Permafrost.* He won the 1998 Appalachian Poetry Contest. His book is *Loan of the Quick* (Sow's Ear Press). **Marge Piercy** is widely published and anthologized. Her awards include a Fellowship from The National Endowment for the Arts, a Carolyn Kizer Poetry Prize, a May Sarton Award, an Arthur C Clark Award, and two honorary doctorates. Her recent books are *The Art of Blessing the Day* (Knopf) and *Early Girl* (Leapfrog Press). "Two Bad You Came In Late" first appeared in *Many Mountains Moving.* **Michael Pollick** is a winner of the Shadyvale Press Chapbook competition and the Showemall's Writer's Block Prize. His poetry has appeared in *Iconoclast, Midwest Poetry Review, Elk River Review, Outlet Poetry Journal* and *Hart.* **Pamela Postai** is the 1998 first place Arkansas Grand Slam winner. **John Potash** is the editor of *Social Justice Action Quarterly.* His work has appeared in *Slant, Penn Review,* and *Falconer.* **Charles Potts** is the author of 17 books including *100 Years in Idaho* (Tsunami Inc) and *How The South Finally Won The Civil War* (Tsunami Inc). He an editor of *The Temple.* **Tarika Powell** is a student at Oberlin College who recently had her first featured reading in Hot Springs, Arkansas. **Rochelle Ratner** is the author of 12 books. She is an editor for *Israel Horizons* and executive editor of *American Book Review.* "Borders" first appeared in *Minnesota Review.* "The Men Talking" first appeared in *Four Zoas.* **David Ray** is the author of several award winning books including *Heartstones: New and Selected Poems* (Micawber Fine Editions) and *Demons in the Diner* (Ashland University Press). His work has appeared in *New Yorker, Nation, Georgia Review, Paris Review, Chicago Review* and *Best American Poetry 1999.* "Back Home" is from *Maharani's Wall.* **Bob Redmond** directs the Seattle Poetry Festival and is managing editor of *Real Change.* His work is in the anthology, *Poetry Nation.* **Terri Rolan** has had poetry in *Outlet Poetry Journal.* **Daniel Roop** has poetry in *Phoenix, Omnivore,* and *Memphis Poetry 40 oz.* "Handing Out Poetry" first appeared in *Monkey.* **James Ruffini** has appeared on WNYU and WFMU radio. He has been published in *Nomad's Choir, Poetalk, Blankgun Silencer* and *Earthbound.* **Thaddeaus Rutkowski** is a Pushcart Prize nominee whose work has appeared in *Columbia Review, Global City Review, Laurel Review, Hart, Outlet Poetry Journal, Stained Sheet* and *Masquerade.* His novel is *Roughhouse* (Kaya). **Felicity Sandburg** has had poetry in *The North Street Journal, Outlet Poetry Journal, Word on the Street,* and *Diner Eucharist.* **Christy Sheffield Sanford** is the author of several books of poetry. Her work has appeared in *Heaven Bone, Cincinnati Poetry Review, Florida Review,* and *Wisconsin Review.* "The Bride's Terrarium, Overgrown" is from her book, *Bride Thrashing Through History*

(Bloody Twin Press). **William Seaton** curates the Poetry on the Loose Reading Series in Middletown. His awards include an Ada Louise Ballard Fellowship and a Helen Fairall Scholarship Award. William has had poetry in *Chelsia*, *Wordsmith*, *Poetry Motel*, *Outlet Poetry Journal* and *North Street Journal* **Sara Seinberg**'s "Fuck You I'm Wonder Woman" appears in audio on the Sister Spit CD, *I Spit on Your Country* (Mouth Almighty). **Reva Sharon** received a grant from the Tel Aviv Foundation of Literary Art. Her work is in *Tel Aviv Review*, *Jerusalem Review*, *Midstream*. Her book is *Pool of the Morning* (Shemesh). "Interlude" first appeared in *ARC, the Journal of the Israel Association of Writers in English*. **David Shevin** is the recipient of fellowships from The NEA and the Ohio Arts Council. His most recent book is *Needles and Needs*. **Ken Siegmann** is a Pulitzer Prize nominated journalist. His poetry is in *Poetic Express*, *Pyrowords*, and *Moondance*; "The Second Coming" is from his book, *The Second Coming and Other Poems* (Toth Press). **Paul Skiff** has had poetry in *Verbal Abuse* and *Aloud: Voices from the Nuyorican Poets Café*. He co-produced *The Nuyorican Symphony* CD, recorded live at The Knitting Factory and is a Rouge Scholar. **Marcus Slease** is an Irish exile living in Utah with work in *Black Bear Review*, *Tule Review*, and *Southern Ocean Review*. **Dave Sloan** has appeared on CNN TV and been published in *Phoenix*, *Gravity Journal*, *Birmingham News* and *The Atlanta Constitution*. **Haigen Smith** has had poetry in *Nerve* and *Hart*. **W. D. Snodgrass**'s first book, *Heart's Needle*, earned him a Pulitzer Prize in 1960. He had received fellowships from The Guggenheim Foundation, The Academy of American Poets, and The National Endowment for the Arts. His poetry has appeared in *American Poetry Review*, *Georgia Review*, *Kenyon Review*, *Michigan Quarterly Review*, and *Seneca Review*. His books include *The Fuehrer Bunker: The Complete Cycle* (BOA Editions). An earlier version of "The Ballad of Jesse Helms" first appeared in *Harvard Review* and appears in *Each In His Season* (BOA Editions). It is used with permission of the publisher. **Katherine Soniat** is on the faculty at Virginia Tech. Her third collection, *A Shared Life*, won the Iowa Prize. Other awards include The William Faulkner Award and a Virginia Commission for the Arts Fellowship. Her poetry has appeared in *Amicus*, *TriQuarterly*, *Gettysburg Review*, *Iowa Review*, *Boulevard*, and *Southern Review*. **Christina Springer** is a Cave Canem Fellow. Her poetry has appeared in *Pennsylvania Review*, *Amethyst*, *Shooting Star Review*, *Mothering Magazine*, and *Outlet Poetry Journal* **Lamont Steptoe** is the author of several books of poetry. His work has appeared in *Painted Bride Quarterly*, *Unity and Struggle*, and *Big Hammer*. "My Song" first appeared in *South Street Star* and appears in his book, *In The Kitchens of the Masters* (Iniquity Press/Vendetta Books). **David Hunter Sutherland** has had poetry in *American Literary Review*, *Owen Wister Review*, and *Oxford University Reader*. **Kyree Swenson** is in *Orange Review*, *Outlet Poetry Journal*, *North Street Journal*, and *Skyscrapers, Taxis, and Tampons* (Fly By Night Press). She directed the theatrical poetry production, *Diner Eucharist*, which was acclaimed by *The Times Herald Record* as one of the ten best shows of 1997. **Alice B Talkless** is in *Longshot* and received a Jackie Go Award. **Susan Tegeler** is literature advisor to The Carroll County Arts Council. Her poetry has appeared in *Diggers Choice*, *Harrisburg Review*, *Baltimore Sunpaper*, *Outlet Poetry Journal*, and *Hart*. Her novel is *Snapdragon* (Brightspot Studios). **Elizabeth Terrazas** has been published in *California Quarterly*. **Hilary Tham** is the author of five books of poetry, the most recent: *Lane with No Name: Memoirs and Poems of A Malaysian-Chinese Girlhood* (Lynne Rienner). Her work has appeared in *Gargoyle* and *Word Wrights*. **Thom World Poet** has twenty chapbooks, and three CDs. He is a co-founder of the Austin International Poetry Festival. **Elizabeth Thomas** is the director of the Words Alive Poetry Project in Connecticut. She is a three time Connecticut team member at the Slam Nationals and was on the USA team in Sweden for the International Slam competition. Her work has appeared in *The Underwood Review*. **Edwin Torres** was the first recipient of the Nuyorican Poets Café Fresh Poet Award in 1991. He has had work in the anthologies *Poetry Nation* and *Aloud: Voices from the Nuyorican Poets Café*. His books include Fractured Humorous (Subpress). His Debut CD is *Holy Kid* (Kill Rockstars Records). **Tusay** writes an arts column for *The Hudson Valley Times*, is editor in chief of *Hart* and a board member of the Newburgh Center for the Arts. His work appears in *Stained Sheets* and *Diner Eucharist* (Orange County Arts Council) An earlier version of "Dismath" appeared in *Hart*. **Charles Vandersee** has had poetry in *Georgia Review, Ohio Review,* and *Poetry*. He teaches at The University of Virginia. **Peter Viereck**'s first book of poetry, *Terror and Decorum* (Scribners) earned him a Pulitzer Prize in 1949. Eight years prior to that, he had released the groundbreaking indictment of the Nazi regime, *Metapolitics: From The Romantics To Hitler* (Knopf). That book has been taught in colleges for close to 60 years. After World War II, it was revised and reissued as *Metapolitics: The Roots of the Nazi Mind*. Peter's awards include fellowships from The Guggenheim Foundation, The Rockefeller Foundation, and the National Endowment for the Arts. His most recent book is *Tide* (University of Arkansas Press, 1995). "History of Revolution" is from his forthcoming book, *Gate Talk*. **Claiborne Schley Walsh** is den mother to all poets. Her poetry has appeared in numerous print and electronic journals. **Bruce Weber** is the editor of *Stained Sheets* and has had poetry in *Rolling Stone* and *Longshot*. His books include *These Poems Are Not Pretty* (Palmetto Press) and *How The Poem Died* (Linear Arts Press) "Toy Soldiers" first appeared in *Hart*. **Scott Wiggerman**'s poetry has appeared in *Black Buzzard Review, Poetry Motel,* and *Paterson Literary Review*. He edited the anthologies *Di-Verse-City* and *Di-Verse-City Too*. **LaVerne Williams** has been published in *A Gathering of the Tribes* and *Phati'tude*. She has received a grant from the Puffin Foundation. **Terry Wright** teaches at the University of Arkansas. The author of two books, Terry's poetry has been published in *Slipstream, Pig Iron,* and *Rolling Stone*. **C. Dale Young** is a physician and associate editor of *New England Review*. His poetry has appeared in *Paris Review, Partisan Review, Southern Review,* and *Yale Review* as well *Best American Poetry 1996*. **Bill Zavatsky** teaches at Trinity School in New York City. His poetry is widely published and anthologized. *Earthlight*, his translations of the poetry of Andre Breton, won the PEN/Book-of-the-Month Club Translation Prize.